"We delight in the beauty of the butterfly, but rarely admit the changes it has gone through to achieve that beauty."

Maya Angelou

This publication is designed to provide accurate and authoritative information in regard to the subject matter covered. It is sold with the understanding that neither the author nor the publisher is engaged in rendering legal, investment, accounting, or other professional services.

While the publisher and author have used their best efforts in preparing this book, they make no representations or warranties with respect to the accuracy or completeness of the contents of this book and specifically disclaim any implied warranties of merchantability or fitness for a particular purpose. No warranty may be created or extended by sales representatives or written sales materials.

The advice and strategies contained herein may not be suitable for your situation.
You should consult with a professional when appropriate. Neither the publisher nor the author shall be liable for any loss of profit or any other commercial damages, including but not limited to special, incidental, consequential, personal, or other damages.

Illustrations by Mary Long

Designed by Tiana Gagic

First edition 2024

ISBN 978-1-7381162-0-1

To the part of you that desires more,
for having the courage to reflect
and the openness to embrace change.

TABLE OF CONTENTS

Welcome Message 6

Introduction: How to Use this Workbook 7

Give Yourself an "A" 8

Part 1: Patterns 11

Awareness: Rewiring Your Brain for Limitless Potential 13

Action: Empower Yourself Through Storytelling 33

Action: Awaken Your Archetypal Energies 38

Love Note: Embracing Discomfort 46

Part 2: Emotions 48

Awareness: Navigating the Intriguing Realm of Human Emotions 52

Action: A Visual Tool for Precise Emotional Awareness 57

Action: Meet Your Human Needs for Emotional Well-being 59

Action: Navigate Emotions with The Change Triangle 64

Action: Uncover the Wisdom Within Emotions 73

Love Note: Befriending Envy 100

Part 3: Boundaries 102

Awareness: Establishing and Upholding Healthy Boundaries 104

Action: Communicating Healthy Boundaries 121

Love Note: Rebuilding Trust 125

Part 4: The Nervous System 127

Awareness: Understanding the Harmonious Dance of Your Nervous Systems 129

Action: Activate Your Vagus Nerve 136

Action: Discover the Power of Breath 138

Action: Alternate Nostril Breathing for Balance and Clarity 140

Action: Renewed Vitality with Breath of Fire 142

Action: Unravel Tension with Progressive Muscle Relaxation 144

Love Note: Rising Above the Flood 147

Part 5: Mindfulness 150
Awareness: Unleash the Power of Mindfulness 152
Action: Mindful of Your Needs 160
Action: Cultivate Present-Moment Awareness 162
Action: Feel Calm and Content 164
Action: Box Breath for Stress and Anxiety Relief 166
Love Note: Embracing Self-Compassion 168

Part 6: Abundance 170
Awareness: Nurturing an Abundant Mindset 172
Action: Cultivate Love and Kindness 178
Action: The Power of Forgiveness and Letting Go 180
Love Note: Shifting Perspectives 182

Part 7: Soul Goals 184
Awareness: An Intentional Journey Toward Alignment 186
Action: Nurture Your Mental Garden 202
Action: Bridging the Gap Between Someday and Today 204
Love Note: Reclaiming My Purpose 206

Additional Tools 208
Embrace the Magic of Gratitude 211
The Art of Holding Space 215
Cultivate Compassion Through Self-love 222
The Power of Positive Affirmations 229
Living a Meaningful Life 238
Access More Joy 243
Movement for Healing 246
The Healing Power of Sound 248
A Letter From Within 250

Book Recommendations 254

About the Author 256

Gratitude from the Author 258

Dear Reader,

Welcome to *Return to You*, a workbook close to my heart as it reflects my mental health journey and the support I received to thrive despite obstacles like anxiety and depression. Most importantly, it's an invitation to explore deep within yourself and use the tools provided to support your own healing and path forward.

During my first year of university, I faced overwhelming anxiety that left me feeling helpless and terrified. I reached out to my family for help and together we tried to understand what was causing such instability in my mental health. This marked the beginning of a series of medical assessments, where doctors prescribed medication without fully grasping my determination to address the underlying causes of my mental health symptoms. These brief appointments left me feeling misunderstood and even more isolated. While I acknowledge the value of medication in managing mental health, it didn't resonate with me then, and I yearned for a different path. So, I embarked on a quest for tools that would help me improve my mental well-being, enabling a life of deeper joy and contentment.

Through this journey, I realized there is no cure for the mental health challenges I experience. However, I discovered powerful tools to manage and thrive despite them. One therapist eloquently compared life to a well-performing stock exchange: although there may be ups and downs, with time and the right tools, the lows won't be as low, and the highs will become higher.

By sharing my story and tools, I aim to provide solace and awareness to others who've experienced the isolating darkness of mental health challenges. My mission is to create a community of acceptance and belonging, where individuals can rediscover their strength and heal together.

This workbook is an opportunity to cultivate an open and curious mindset, allowing you to explore new avenues of self-discovery and growth. Approach these concepts with an open mind, accepting or rejecting them as you desire. The choice is always yours, and I respect and honor your individuality.

With gratitude and love,

N Harrison

How to use this workbook

Within this workbook, you will explore seven areas that contribute to your well-being when nurtured: Patterns, Emotions, Boundaries, The Nervous System, Mindfulness, Abundance, and Soul Goals. Follow the recommended order and commit to completing each section before proceeding to the next. Use the carefully crafted four-step process and aim to inspire self-awareness and personal growth.

Step 1: Awaken

Each section begins with an inspiring quote as your catalyst. It was chosen to awaken a dormant energy within you and create a desire for self-exploration.

Step 2: Awareness

You will delve into concepts that hold significance in your life. Through thought-provoking exercises and insightful journal prompts, you will aim to generate a deeper awareness of how these concepts manifest and can blossom in your experiences.

Step 3: Action

With newfound awareness, you'll uncover tools that empower you to take action and implement this work. These tools serve as a roadmap for personal growth, enabling you to implement positive changes and navigate challenges that may arise. Choose the tools you find most helpful.

Step 4: Love Notes

I vulnerably share my journey and the profound shifts that have unfolded for me by completing this work. This intimate reflection will hopefully serve as a gentle reminder that you are not alone on this courageous journey.

Trust yourself and your intuitive instincts on this journey. Embrace the discomfort of change, and celebrate the victories. If you feel overwhelmed, struggle with uncomfortable feelings, or need personalized support, I strongly recommend that you seek the guidance of a mental health professional.

GIVE YOURSELF AN "A" BEFORE YOU BEGIN

According to Ben Zander, adopting an "A" mindset before starting something new can be a game-changer in achieving success. By doing so, you acknowledge your potential and ability to excel without needing external validation or approval. This mindset enables a positive and confident attitude, empowering you to fully commit to your goals and face challenges with determination. It signifies a belief in your capabilities and a commitment to excellence. Take a moment to reflect on these journal prompts and discover how it feels to trust your ability to thrive on this journey, even before it begins.

Reflect on your upcoming Return to You journey. How could adopting an “A” mindset change your perspective and attitude toward completing it?

Where in your life do you seek external validation before fully committing to a goal? How might embracing an “A” mindset impact your ability to succeed?

Imagine if you gave yourself an "A" in all aspects of your life. How would this mindset influence your daily actions, decision-making, and happiness?

Write a letter from your future self. You've just received an "A" after completing the Return To You workbook. Describe how it feels to receive the "A" and what you did to achieve the positive outcome.

PATTERNS

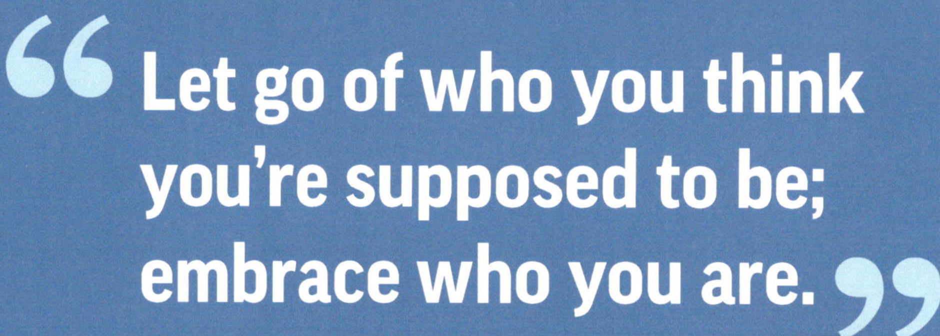
"Let go of who you think
you're supposed to be;
embrace who you are."

Brené Brown

AWARENESS

REWIRING YOUR BRAIN FOR **LIMITLESS POTENTIAL**

As you interact with your surroundings, your brain analyzes the information and establishes links between neurons, known as synapses. These synapses facilitate the flow of information throughout your brain.

The young child's brain is particularly receptive to forming these connections, facilitating cognitive development. When you experience something important or potentially dangerous, your brain strengthens the associations between your thoughts and emotions. These established connections are commonly referred to as patterns or beliefs. As you age, these patterns become automatic and influence your thoughts, emotions, and behaviours without you consciously realizing it. Over time, these patterns may no longer be helpful and become limiting patterns.

To change limiting patterns, you must become aware of them and actively engage in new thoughts. By challenging and replacing old limiting patterns, you can form new connections and strengthen different neural pathways in your brain. With repeated practice, these new pathways become more established, allowing you to form new and more beneficial patterns of thinking and behaving.

Below are several examples of common patterns and how they can be limiting:

SELF-DOUBT:

Constantly questioning your abilities, second-guessing decisions, and feeling inadequate or incapable.

PERFECTIONISM:

Setting excessively high standards for yourself, being overly critical of mistakes, and feeling anxious or stressed when things aren't perfect.

PROCRASTINATION:

Delaying tasks or responsibilities, often due to fear of failure, overwhelm, or lack of motivation.

PEOPLE-PLEASING:

Constantly seeking approval or validation from others, prioritizing others' needs over your own, and fearing rejection or conflict.

NEGATIVE SELF-TALK:

Engaging in self-critical or self-deprecating thoughts, focusing on weaknesses or failures, and lacking self-compassion or self-acceptance.

FEAR OF FAILURE:

Avoiding risks or challenges, staying within comfort zones, and feeling anxious or paralyzed when faced with potential failure.

COMPARISON:

Constantly comparing yourself to others, feeling inadequate or envious, and basing self-worth on external achievements or appearances.

OVERTHINKING:

Overanalyzing situations, obsessively worrying about the future, and getting stuck in a cycle of indecision or rumination.

APPROVAL-SEEKING:

Constantly seeking approval from others, basing self-worth on external validation, and feeling insecure when not receiving it.

AVOIDANCE:

Avoiding uncomfortable or challenging situations, conflicts, or emotions and resorting to distractions or escapism.

SELF-SABOTAGE:

Engaging in behaviours or making choices that undermine personal success or well-being, often due to fear of success, change, or low self-esteem.

CATASTROPHIZING:

Exaggerating or magnifying negative outcomes or situations, expecting the worst-case scenario, and feeling overwhelmed or anxious.

CONTROL:

Trying to control every aspect or situation in life, feeling anxious or stressed when things are uncertain or out of control, and struggling to delegate or trust others.

VICTIM MENTALITY:

Perceiving yourself as a perpetual victim, blaming external circumstances or others for personal problems, and feeling helpless or powerless.

OVERWORKING:

Constantly overloading yourself with tasks and responsibilities, neglecting self-care or personal relationships, and feeling burnt out or exhausted.

PEOPLE-AVOIDANCE:

Avoiding social interactions or isolating oneself, often due to social anxiety, fear of judgment, or discomfort in social settings.

FIXED MINDSET:

Believing that abilities, intelligence, or skills are fixed traits that cannot be developed or improved, often leading to a fear of failure or resistance to learning.

IMPOSTER SYNDROME:

Feeling like a fraud or believing that your achievements are undeserved, discounting success as luck or due to external factors, and fearing being exposed as incompetent.

Below are examples of how these common patterns can benefit you:

SELF-DOUBT:

Questioning your abilities can serve you by encouraging self-reflection and committing to personal growth. It pushes you to challenge yourself and seek improvement.

PERFECTIONISM:

Setting high standards for yourself can motivate you to strive for excellence. It emphasizes attention to detail and ensures a commitment to producing quality work.

PROCRASTINATION:

It can serve as a signal that something is not aligned with your values or goals. It provides an opportunity to reflect on priorities and make necessary adjustments.

PEOPLE-PLEASING:

Seeking validation from others can promote empathy and consideration for others' needs. It can foster harmonious relationships and create a supportive community.

APPROVAL-SEEKING:

Seeking validation from others can enhance your understanding of different perspectives and improve your interpersonal skills. It can also create an environment of collaboration.

NEGATIVE SELF-TALK:

Engaging in self-critical thoughts can serve as a catalyst for personal growth. It motivates you to identify areas for improvement and develop resilience in the face of adversity.

FEAR OF FAILURE:

Avoiding risks can keep you grounded and prevent impulsive decision-making. It can also drive you to analyze situations and plan effectively.

COMPARISON:

Comparing yourself to others can provide inspiration for personal growth. It can also highlight areas where you can strive to improve and set higher goals.

OVERTHINKING:

Analyzing situations can improve problem-solving skills and enhance decision-making. It can also encourage self-reflection.

VICTIM MENTALITY:

Identifying external factors can provide insight into patterns and triggers. It allows for introspection and empowers you to take responsibility and make positive changes.

AVOIDANCE:

Avoiding uncomfortable situations protects your mental and emotional well-being. It can also serve as a reminder to prioritize self-care and boundaries.

SELF-SABOTAGE:

Recognizing self-sabotaging behaviours prompts the need for self-reflection and personal growth. It highlights areas where healing and self-compassion are needed.

CATASTROPHIZING:

Preparing for worst-case scenarios can lead to proactive problem-solving and contingency planning. It also highlights potential risks and encourages preparedness.

CONTROL:

Striving for control can foster discipline and organization, increasing productivity and efficiency. It can also create a sense of stability and reduce anxiety in uncertain situations.

OVERWORKING:

Being dedicated to tasks and responsibilities demonstrates a strong work ethic. It can lead to personal and professional growth and create opportunities for success.

PEOPLE-AVOIDANCE:

Taking time for solitude can promote introspection and self-reflection. It can also allow for relaxation and rejuvenation, contributing to personal well-being.

FIXED MINDSET:

Recognizing a fixed mindset opens opportunities for a growth mindset. Embracing a growth mindset can lead to continuous learning, resilience, and personal development.

IMPOSTER SYNDROME:

Feeling like a fraud indicates a drive for improvement and a desire to excel. It can motivate you to seek additional knowledge or skills to increase self-confidence.

Examine the patterns in your life.

Create a list of the patterns you notice within yourself. Identify all the patterns that relate to you, even if they have not been mentioned. Reflect on the benefits and limitations these patterns bring to your life.

Example

Pattern One: *Control*

How does this pattern limit you?

As a small business owner, delivering an exceptional member experience is crucial. My strong desire for control motivates me to establish stringent quality control measures, ensuring that each experience in the studio is positive for our members.

How your pattern limits you:

My controlling pattern can inadvertently stifle the trainer's creativity and hinder our team's ability to innovate. I must recognize how my need for control impacts the people I value. It is imperative that I grant them the freedom they require to infuse their unique offering into our class experiences.

PATTERN ONE:

How does this pattern benefit you?

How does this pattern limit you?

PATTERN TWO:

How does this pattern benefit you?

How does this pattern limit you?

PATTERN THREE:

How does this pattern benefit you?

How does this pattern limit you?

PATTERN FOUR:

How does this pattern benefit you?

How does this pattern limit you?

PATTERN FIVE:

How does this pattern benefit you?

How does this pattern limit you?

Realize the cost of holding onto your limiting beliefs and remain committed.

You can determine if a pattern limits or benefits you by paying attention to how you feel in your body. When you feel positive emotions, it indicates that the pattern is beneficial. On the other hand, negative emotions serve as a signal for you to shift your thoughts and distance yourself from the pattern intentionally.

The process of changing a limiting pattern requires reflection and courage. It may involve questioning ingrained beliefs and feeling uncomfortable at times. Nevertheless, the rewards of breaking free from limiting patterns are significant. By changing your patterns, you can cultivate healthier and more satisfying relationships and open yourself up to new possibilities.

Choose one pattern that currently feels very limiting in your life. Imagine yourself five years from now without making any changes to your limiting pattern. Reflect on the potential consequences and challenges that may arise if this pattern remains unchanged.

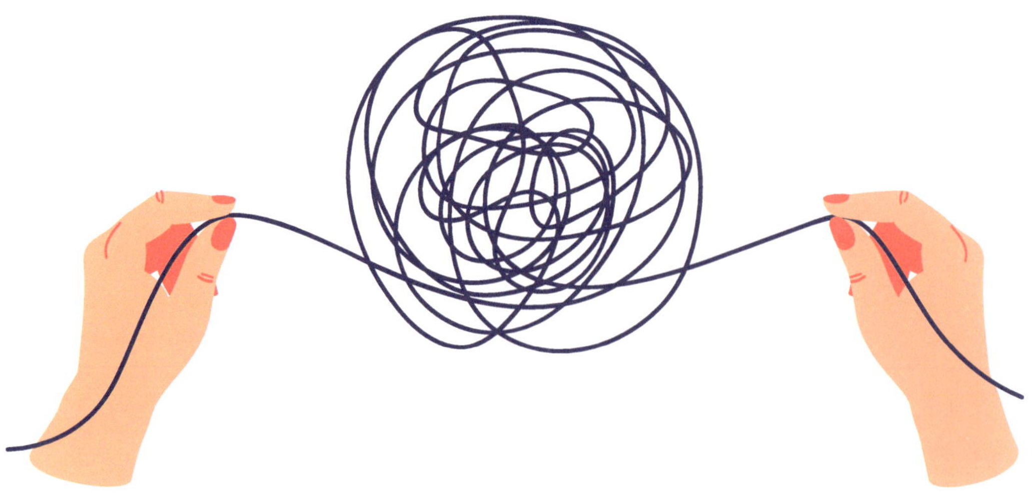

ENDEAVOURS

How could this pattern impact your professional growth or personal endeavours? Reflect on the potential missed opportunities, stagnation, or lack of fulfillment that could occur if the pattern remains unchanged.

WELL-BEING

Consider the potential impact on your physical, mental, and emotional well-being. Reflect on how this limiting pattern may lead to increased stress, unhealthy habits, neglect of self-care, or even physical ailments if left unchanged.

CONNECTION TO SELF

Consider how this pattern may impact your spiritual or inner life. Reflect on the potential disconnection, lack of meaning, or feelings of emptiness that could arise if you neglect this aspect of your life.

CREATIVITY AND LEARNING

Explore how this pattern might hinder your personal growth, creativity, and sense of contentment. Reflect on the missed opportunities for learning, self-discovery, and pursuing your passions that may arise if this limiting pattern continues.

RELATIONSHIPS

Explore how this pattern might affect your relationships with family, friends, romantic partners, or colleagues. Reflect on the potential strain, conflicts, or lack of fulfillment that could arise, hindering your ability to build and maintain healthy and meaningful connections.

Common barriers you may encounter.

Acknowledging potential barriers is an essential step toward making positive changes in your patterns. It allows your mind to better understand your challenges and explore ways to overcome them.

LACK OF MOTIVATION:

Staying motivated can be difficult, especially when changing old patterns that feel comfortable and familiar. To overcome this, remind yourself why you want to change and the benefits it will bring. Setting achievable goals and celebrating small victories will boost motivation.

LIMITED SUPPORT:

Sometimes, you may lack the necessary support from others to make the desired changes. Connecting with like-minded individuals, joining support groups, or seeking professional help can provide the proper support for you.

FEAR OF FAILURE:

Fear of failure can often hold you back from making changes. It's important to remember that setbacks are a natural part of the learning process and provide valuable growth opportunities. Embracing a growth mindset and viewing challenges as learning experiences can help overcome this barrier.

HABITS AND ROUTINES:

Breaking old habits and establishing new ones can be challenging. One way to overcome this is by gradually creating a plan to replace old patterns with new ones. Implementing reminders, and seeking accountability from a friend can also help make changes stick.

NEGATIVE SELF-TALK:

Your thoughts can sometimes become barriers to change. Challenging and reframing negative self-talk with positive affirmations, or seeking guidance from positive people can help overcome this barrier.

What obstacles do you foresee as you embark on the journey of unravelling old limiting patterns and forging new ones? Reflect on strategies to overcome these challenges through your journaling.

SUMMARY

The plasticity of your brain enables change and new learning to occur by forming new connections between neurons and modifying existing ones. The process of rewiring your brain for unlimited potential involves recognizing and changing limiting patterns that have become deeply ingrained in your subconscious. These patterns, such as self-doubt, perfectionism, and fear of failure, may have benefits in certain situations but can ultimately hinder your personal growth as an adult. By consciously acknowledging and actively engaging in new thoughts and behaviours, you can forge new connections and reinforce different pathways in your brain, ultimately establishing more beneficial patterns.

It is helpful to share this work with someone you trust and to ask for their support. Whenever you recognize a pattern that is not benefiting you, take a moment to pause and consider using the tools provided in the following pages. These tools are designed to help you shift your perspective and embrace thoughts that will serve you better.

EMPOWER YOURSELF THROUGH STORYTELLING

Stories shape our understanding of the world and give our lives meaning. They have a stronger impact on memory and learning than plain facts or data because they engage multiple brain regions and enhance attention and recall. Moreover, stories influence our emotions, decision-making, self-perception, beliefs, attitudes, and behaviours. The narratives we tell ourselves can either empower us or hold us back. To break free from limiting old patterns, we need to step back, assess the situation, and consciously create a new story or meaning. By doing so, we can make better choices, develop new patterns, and find personal growth and development. Recognizing tension and discomfort is a sign that a more positive story is waiting for us.

Journal about an experience that triggered strong emotions and caused discomfort. Include as many details as you can remember, including how you felt, the people involved, where it happened, what was said, or not, and any other relevant information.

Identify all the facts that occurred during this situation. Facts are devoid of personal opinions, interpretations, or biases. By removing subjective elements and focusing on facts, you can present a clear and accurate account of the event that took place.

Describe all the emotions you felt during and after this experience using the Feelings Wheel on page 58 if needed.

What pattern was triggered during this experience, and what story or interpretation did you create regarding this event? What meaning (about yourself) did you attach to this experience?

Rewrite the story or meaning you initially assigned this experience. Focus on the facts and create a new narrative that empowers you. Take a deep cleansing breath in and out of your body and repeat: I am willing to see this differently.

AWAKEN YOUR ARCHETYPAL ENERGIES

As you become aware of restricting patterns and make efforts to transition into ways of being that benefit you, refer to Archetypal Energies for insight into your authentic self. Archetypal energy refers to the universal patterns and qualities that exist within every individual. These energies are timeless and have been passed down through generations, shaping your attitudes, behaviours, and perceptions. By becoming aware of these inner archetypal energies, you can gain deeper insight into your true self and develop a greater self-awareness.

Here are five common Archetypal energies that you may find yourself able to connect and resonate with:

THE HERO:

The Hero archetype represents strength, bravery, and the desire to overcome obstacles and achieve greatness. This energy is characterized by determination, resilience, and a strong sense of purpose.

THE LOVER:

The Lover archetype embodies passion, intimacy, and emotional connection. This energy is characterized by love, sensuality, and the pursuit of deep relationships and experiences.

THE SAGE:

The Sage archetype represents wisdom, knowledge, and intellectual curiosity. This energy is characterized by a thirst for learning, analytical thinking, and a desire to understand the world and its mysteries.

THE MAGICIAN:

The Magician archetype symbolizes transformation, creativity, and the ability to manifest desires. This energy is characterized by a deep connection to intuition, the power to shape reality, and the pursuit of spiritual growth.

THE JESTER:

The Jester archetype embodies humour, playfulness, and the ability to bring joy and laughter into the world. This energy encourages people to embrace their inner child, let go of seriousness, and find happiness in the present moment.

When you recognize and appreciate the values and behaviours in others, you validate those qualities within yourself. By embracing these qualities, you can break free from old limiting patterns. This empowering practice allows you to live in harmony with your true self, giving you clarity, purpose, and fulfillment as you navigate life. Use the journal prompts to help you uncover dormant archetypal energies within you. Enjoy the journey of discovering and connecting with your authentic self through the exploration of these energies.

Explore a time when you felt a strong connection to these archetypal energies within yourself. What were the qualities and characteristics that emerged during that experience?

Reflect on the people you admire in your life. Contemplate the values, beliefs, and behaviours they exemplify, and delve into how these admirable qualities also exist within you.

Identify a limiting belief or conditioned pattern that hinders your progress or prevents you from living authentically. How might embracing these energies help you live in alignment with your true self?

Imagine yourself fully embracing and integrating your archetypal energies. How would your life look and feel? What opportunities would open up for you?

Take a moment to explore the layers that make up your authentic self. What archetypal energies do you sense within you? How do these energies contribute to your sense of identity and purpose?

Reflect on a time when you felt a deep sense of authenticity and fulfillment. What archetypal energies were present during that experience?

LOVE NOTE

A Love Note on Embracing Discomfort

Ask anyone who knows me, and they'll affirm that I am typically brimming with optimism. I firmly believe that we possess the capability to accomplish anything we dedicate our minds to. Nonetheless, there have been occasions where I find myself devoid of such optimism.

For a long time, I've dreamt of writing a memoir about my journey with anxiety. When I finally felt ready to begin, I created a comprehensive book proposal. I sought out a writing coach to support me along this intimidating journey, especially since I didn't have much experience in writing. Unfortunately, after a few months of working together, we hadn't made the progress I had hoped for, and we decided to go our separate ways. My coach confessed that she didn't have the time to provide the support I needed, and she gave me a list of coaches who might be able to help me.

As soon as the call ended, my lower lip quivered, and tears welled up in my eyes. Deep down, I knew it was the right decision, but I felt incredibly alone and crushed. I turned to my journal, as I typically do when seeking clarity or processing strong emotions.

I listed the facts of the situation:

- I want to write a book.
- My current writing coach is too busy.
- I need a new source of support.

Then, I wrote out all the ugly mess inside my head, the meaning and story I was attaching to these facts:

- I am nowhere near good enough to even consider having a dream as big as this.
- It's clear that I should give up on this book. Quitting is the only option.
- Who do I think I am, having the audacity to believe I am even remotely worthy of being called an author?
- My story isn't worthy of publication.
- She has time, but I'm a terrible writer and no one can help me.
- I am such a failure; there is no point in continuing to write.

As I wrote down these negative thoughts, I realized I had fallen into my familiar victim pattern. Unconsciously, this pattern had been whispering words that sparked a sense of unworthiness within me. I didn't like how this pattern made me feel, so I kept journaling to see what else was available. This time, I shifted my attention to the true nature of what was going on inside my head.

- I am creating this negative meaning.
- It's not serving me or helping me achieve my goals.
- I am enrolling myself in a victim story and feel discouraged.
- I can choose to stay in this mindset or shift my perspective.
- I am responsible for my feelings and the actions I take.
- I have the ability to empower myself with new options and opportunities.

By recognizing the facts of my situation and not getting caught up in the negative meaning my pattern had created, I could align myself with empowering next steps instead of drowning in discouragement. This allowed me to let go of the victim pattern I often defaulted to and instead choose actions that propelled my journey forward.

Despite my optimism returning, I still felt vulnerable and tender as I pursued writing my memoir. And maybe that was exactly where I needed to be. In my SAOR classes, I always urged people to step out of their comfort zones because that's where growth happens. I embraced the discomfort, registered for a non-fiction writing course at the University of Toronto, and, most importantly, kept writing.

EMOTIONS

“Between the stimulus and response, there is a space. And in that space lies our freedom and power to choose our responses. In our response lies our growth and our freedom.”

Viktor Frankl

AWARENESS

NAVIGATING THE INTRIGUING REALM OF **HUMAN EMOTIONS**

Emotions play a fundamental role in shaping your human experience, and gaining a deeper understanding of them can pave the way for more intelligent emotional navigation. Acting as your guide, emotions offer invaluable insights into yourself and your environment. They function as signals, helping you make sense of your experiences and directing your actions accordingly. For instance, feelings of fear can alert you to potential threats, prompting you to take necessary precautions. On the other hand, sensations of joy may point out activities that bring you true happiness and fulfillment.

Your emotions serve as valuable sources of information about your needs, values, and boundaries. Trusting them can lead you toward what truly matters to you. By practicing self-compassion and fully embracing your emotions, you can navigate life authentically, aligning with your deepest values.

It's important to recognize that emotions alone should not be the sole basis for decision-making. Rational thinking and logical considerations hold their importance. Striking a balance between emotions and rationality allows for a more holistic understanding of yourself and the world.

The next time you sense an emotion swelling within you, create a safe space for yourself; allow it to surface and be fully experienced. Use the following journal prompts to uncover the available wisdom and navigate your path forward.

Describe the emotion you are currently feeling. What physical sensations are associated with it? Where do you feel it in your body?

What triggered this emotion? Was it a specific event, interaction, or thought? Write about the circumstances surrounding the feeling.

Are there certain situations or people that consistently evoke this emotion? What could this tell you about your values or boundaries?

Are there any past experiences that might be influencing your current emotional response? Reflect on how these past experiences might be shaping your present emotions and behaviours.

What self-care practices can support you in processing and managing this emotion? How can you show yourself compassion and kindness during this time?

What is this emotion trying to tell you? Consider any potential actions or changes you can make to honour and address this emotion.

SUMMARY

Emotions are important signals, providing valuable information about yourself and your surroundings. They guide your behaviour and decision-making, and it is crucial to recognize and acknowledge all emotions. Emotions offer insights into your needs, values, and boundaries, and trusting them can help you make authentic choices. Self-compassion is essential when facing difficult emotions. However, emotions should not be the sole basis for decision-making, as rational thinking is also important.

The next time you feel an emotion rising, use the journal prompts to welcome the feeling and the tools in the next section to process it fully. Reviewing the Feelings Wheel, understanding your human needs, and navigating The Change Triangle help you better understand and embrace your emotions, leading to a more authentic and value-aligned life focused on well-being.

ACTION

A VISUAL TOOL FOR PRECISE EMOTIONAL AWARENESS

A Feelings Wheel is a visual tool that helps you identify and understand your emotions. It categorizes emotions into levels, allowing for more precise emotional awareness. To use it, identify your primary emotion at the center, explore the related secondary sensations, and refine to a more specific feeling. This tool promotes emotional intelligence, self-awareness, and effective communication.

Feelings Wheel

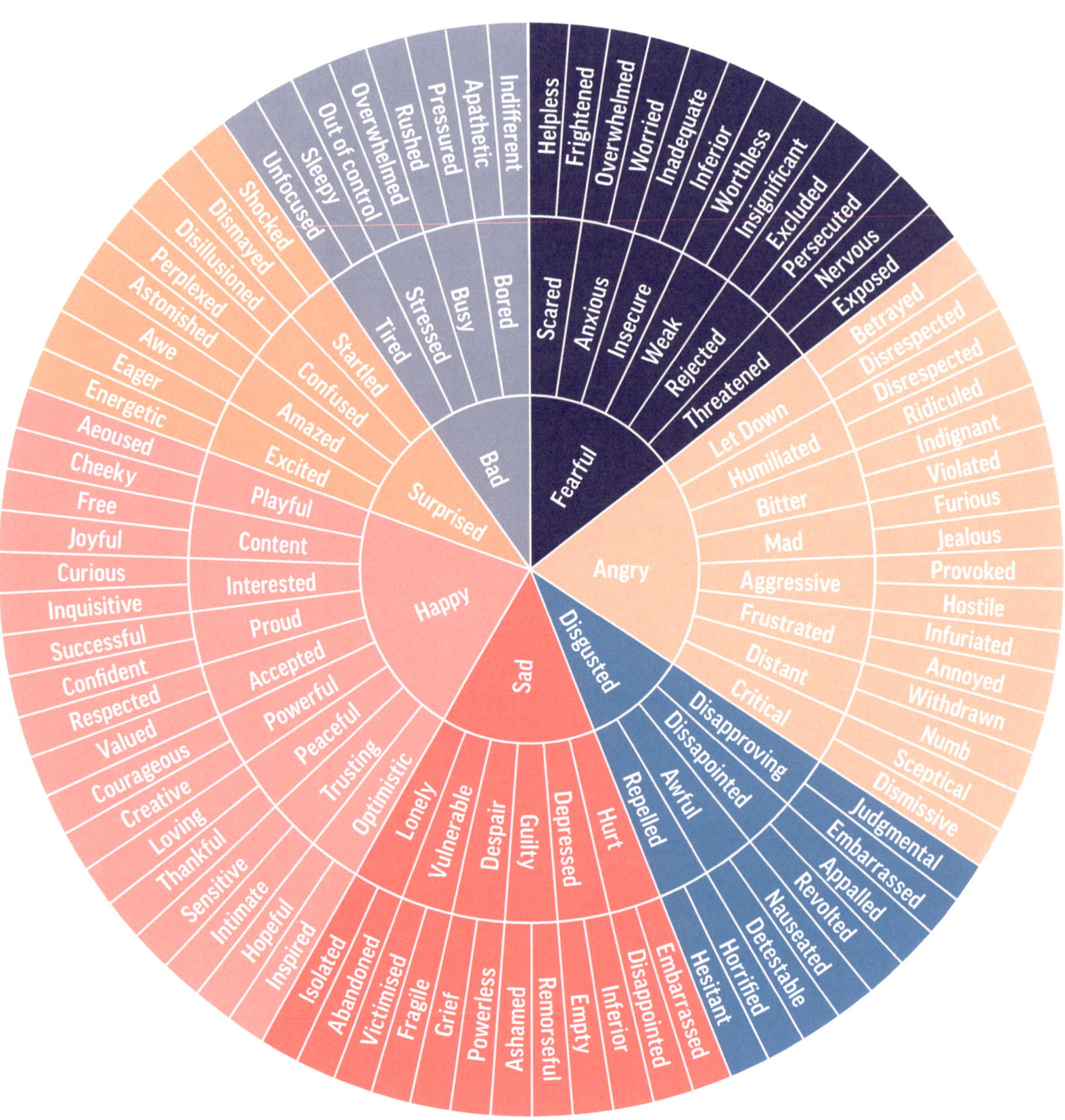

Originally created by Dr. Gloria Wilcox

ACTION

MEET YOUR HUMAN NEEDS FOR EMOTIONAL WELL-BEING

In part one of this workbook, you learned how your past experiences, background, and culture can shape your patterns. When you become aware of these patterns, you can evaluate whether they align with who you are and make necessary adjustments. Your patterns shape your needs. If you are in a controlling pattern, you need control of your environment.

Understanding your needs allows you to make better decisions, set boundaries, and prioritize your well-being. You feel content, joyful, and satisfied when your needs are met. When your needs go unfulfilled, you can feel overwhelmed with unpleasant emotions.

Below is a list of common human needs.

Check the ones that, if they become unmet, trigger an emotional response within you.

RESPECT:
The need to be treated with dignity and honour.

PEACEFULNESS:
The need for tranquility and a calm environment.

BELONGING:
The need to feel connected, accepted, and included in social groups.

AUTONOMY:
The need for independence and the freedom to choose.

SECURITY:
The need for safety, both physically and emotionally.

AUTHENTICITY:
The need to be true to oneself and live in alignment with personal values.

PREDICTABILITY:
The need for stability and a sense of routine.

SELF-EXPRESSION:
The need to express oneself creatively and authentically.

LOVE:
The need for affection, care, and emotional intimacy.

TRUST:
The need to have faith in others and believe in their reliability.

RECOGNITION:
The need to be acknowledged and appreciated for contributions.

LEARNING:
The need for intellectual growth, acquiring knowledge, and expanding skills.

SOLITUDE:
The need for personal space and time alone for reflection and rejuvenation.

MEANING:
The need to find purpose and significance in life.

ADVENTURE:
The need for excitement, exploration, and new experiences.

EMPATHY:
The need to understand and share the feelings of others.

FAIRNESS:
The need for justice, equality, and fairness in treatment.

PHYSICAL WELL-BEING:
The need for good health, exercise, and nutrition.

EMOTIONAL WELL-BEING:
The need for emotional balance, self-care, and stress management.

INTIMACY:
The need for deep emotional and physical closeness with others.

BELIEF:
The need for a sense of faith, spirituality, or connection to something greater.

CREATIVITY:
The need for self-expression through artistic or innovative endeavours.

SUPPORT:
The need for encouragement, assistance, and a reliable support system.

HARMONY:
The need for peaceful relationships and a sense of unity.

ACHIEVEMENT:
The need for accomplishment, growth, and reaching personal goals.

FREEDOM:
The need for release from constraints and limitations.

FUN:
The need for enjoyment, playfulness, and lightheartedness.

CONNECTION:
The need for social interaction, companionship, and a sense of community.

CLARITY:
The need for clear communication, understanding, and transparency.

GRATITUDE:
The need to appreciate and express gratitude for the blessings in one's life.

Reflect on a moment when you experienced a strong emotional response or felt triggered. Elaborate on the events that unfolded during this event.

Explore the Feelings Wheel on page 58 to identify the exact emotions you experienced. How do these emotions manifest physically?

Was an old pattern activated during this particular moment? Was there an unmet need in this situation? If so, why does meeting this need hold significance for you?

With this new awareness surrounding your needs, what potential choices or boundaries could you establish to prioritize your overall well-being?

NAVIGATE EMOTIONS WITH THE CHANGE TRIANGLE

The Change Triangle was developed by Hilary Jacobs Hendel, a psychotherapist, and is based on Accelerated Experiential Dynamic Psychotherapy (AEDP) principles. My therapist introduced me to this powerful tool, which helped guide me through overwhelming anxiety.

The Change Triangle is designed to help individuals navigate and understand their emotions. It focuses on three key components: defences, inhibitory emotions and core emotions. The Change Triangle emphasizes the importance of connecting with and feeling your core emotions, recognizing the defences you use to protect yourself from them, and understanding the inhibitory emotions that may be blocking them. By working through these components, you can develop emotional resilience, self-awareness, and healthier ways of relating to yourself and others.

Change Triangle

Defense

BEING BUSY
SCROLLING
DRINKING
EATING

Inhibitor

SHAME
ANXIETY
GUILT

Core Emotion

SADNESS, FEAR, ANGER, JOY, EXCITEMENT, SEXUAL EXCITEMENT, DISGUST

OPENHEARTED STATE

CALM, CURIOUS, CONNECTED, CONFIDENT, COURAGEOUS, CLEAR

Understanding the Change Triangle

In order to gain a deeper understanding of the Change Triangle, take some time to familiarize yourself with the descriptions of each component. Afterwards, make use of the journal prompts provided to effectively navigate your emotions and foster a mindset of openness and acceptance.

DEFENCE:

Defences are protective mechanisms your mind and body employ to shield you from overwhelming emotions. They are unconscious strategies you use to manage distress and maintain a sense of control. Common defences include denial, avoidance, intellectualizing, rationalizing, and distracting yourself from your emotions. Defences can be helpful in the short term, but they often prevent you from fully experiencing and processing your emotions, leading to increased stress and anxiety.

INHIBITORY EMOTIONS:

Inhibitory emotions are secondary emotions that arise as a result of defences. They act as a barrier between your intellect and core emotions, preventing you from fully experiencing them. Inhibitory emotions include anxiety, shame, and guilt. These emotions often serve as a protective layer, allowing you to keep your core emotions hidden to avoid the discomfort that may arise from facing them.

CORE EMOTIONS:

Core emotions are primary, universal emotions that are essential to your human experience. They include joy, sadness, fear, anger, disgust, and surprise. Core emotions are instinctive and provide important information about your needs, desires, and experiences. They are often intense and can be uncomfortable, but they are essential for your emotional well-being. By embracing your core emotions, you can gain valuable insights about yourself and lead you to an openhearted state.

OPENHEARTED STATE:

Open-Heart state is a desired emotional state characterized by compassion, connection, and vulnerability. It involves being open to experiencing and expressing emotions authentically, fostering deep connections and empathy in relationships. You can access an Open-Heart state only when you have experienced your core emotions.

DEFENCES

What are some common defences you rely on to avoid feeling uncomfortable emotions?

How do these defences protect you?

DEFENCES

Can you identify any underlying fears or beliefs that contribute to these defences?

How can you recognize and challenge these defences when they arise so you can move past them?

INHIBITORY EMOTIONS

What inhibitory emotions, such as shame, guilt or anxiety, tend to hold you back in life?

How do these inhibitory emotions manifest in your thoughts, behaviours, or decision-making process?

INHIBITORY EMOTIONS

What are the underlying beliefs or past experiences that contribute to these inhibitory emotions?

How can you develop strategies to acknowledge and manage these inhibitory emotions in a healthy way?

CORE EMOTIONS

Which core emotions provoke defensive or inhibitory responses, warning you to avoid them?

What practices can you explore to express these core emotions constructively instead of blocking them?

OPENHEARTED STATE

What kind of emotional freedom can you experience by going through this process?

How could your life expand and improve if you regularly embraced The Change Triangle process?

ACTION

UNCOVER THE WISDOM WITHIN EMOTIONS

Taking the time to feel and explore your emotions is essential because it enhances self-awareness, emotional intelligence, and personal growth. By fully experiencing and acknowledging your emotions, you gain valuable insights into yourself, your needs, and your values. This self-awareness helps you make informed decisions, handle conflicts better, and build healthier relationships.

Review these shared emotions and the wisdom that may be available from processing them fully. When you experience one of these emotions, pause and use the journal prompts to help you explore insights and identify any necessary actions.

ANGER:

Anger often signifies a perceived injustice or boundary violation. It may indicate a need to assert yourself, establish boundaries, or address the source of your anger in a constructive manner.

JOY:

Joy typically indicates a positive emotional state and can signify fulfillment, happiness, or contentment. Embrace and savour joyful moments, as they can enhance well-being and inspire a sense of gratitude.

GRIEF:

Grief can be a response to loss, disappointment, or sadness. It may indicate a need for selfcare, support from others, or processing and healing through activities like journaling or talking to a therapist.

FEAR:

Fear often arises as a response to perceived threats or danger. It may indicate a need for self-protection or caution. Assess the situation and take appropriate steps to ensure your safety or address underlying concerns.

LOVE:

Love represents deep affection, connection, or attachment to someone or something. It may suggest a need for nurturing relationships, expressing gratitude, or acts of kindness toward others.

GUILT:

Guilt arises when you believe you have disrupted your moral code. It can prompt you to apologize or make amends. Reflect on the situation, learn from it, and take appropriate action to address any harm caused.

SHAME:

Shame arises from feelings of inadequacy or self-judgment. It can indicate a need for self-compassion, self-acceptance, or seeking reassurance and support from others.

EXCITEMENT:

Excitement signifies enthusiasm, anticipation, or eagerness. It can inspire motivation, action, or pursue new opportunities. Embrace the energy and channel it into productive endeavours.

SURPRISE:

Surprise is a sudden reaction to unexpected events or information. It can prompt curiosity, exploration, or adaptation to new circumstances. Embrace the opportunity to learn, grow, or adjust your plans accordingly.

JEALOUSY:

Jealousy signals that you might have unfulfilled desires, insecurities, or areas for personal growth. Exploring this emotion can offer valuable insights into your own aspirations and help you understand what you truly want.

DISGUST:

Disgust is often triggered by things that are offensive or repulsive to you. It can indicate a need to distance yourself from certain situations, behaviours, or individuals that are harmful or incompatible with your values.

ENVY:

Envy is an emotion that arises when we desire qualities or possessions that others have. It serves as a signal, highlighting areas where we feel unfulfilled. By paying attention to our envy, we can gain insight into our own desires and values.

ANGER

What specific event or situation triggered your anger?

Was there a boundary or value that was disregarded?

ANGER

How could you assert yourself or communicate your needs effectively in this situation?

What constructive actions could you take to address the source of your anger?

What specific event or experience brought you joy?

What aspects of this experience resonate deeply with you?

How can you incorporate more of these elements into your life?

What actions can you take to share or spread this joy with others?

GRIEF

What specific event or loss triggered your grief?

What emotions or thoughts arise when you sit with your grief?

GRIEF

How can you honour and process this grief in a healthy way?

What actions can you take to support your healing and well-being during this time?

FEAR

What specific situation or circumstance is causing you fear?

What are the underlying beliefs or thoughts contributing to this fear?

FEAR

What steps can you take to address or mitigate the source of your fear?

How can you support yourself in feeling safe and secure?

LOVE

Who or what is the object of your love and affection?

What qualities or aspects of this person or thing do you appreciate most?

LOVE

How can you express and nurture this love in your relationships?

What actions can you take to cultivate more love and connection in your life?

What specific action or event is causing you guilt?

What values or standards do you feel you have disregarded?

GUILT

How can you take responsibility for your actions and make amends if necessary?

What actions can you take to prevent similar situations in the future?

SHAME

What specific event or circumstance triggered your feelings of shame?

What underlying beliefs or judgments are contributing to this shame?

SHAME

How can you practice self-compassion and self-acceptance in this situation?

What actions can you take to challenge and reframe these negative beliefs?

DISGUST

What specific situation or behaviour is triggering your disgust?

What values or principles do you feel are being compromised?

DISGUST

How can you distance yourself from these situations or behaviours?

What actions can you take to align more closely with your values?

SURPRISE

What specific event or information took you by surprise?

What emotions or thoughts arise when you reflect on this surprise?

SURPRISE

How can you embrace and adapt to this new circumstance or information?

What actions can you take to explore or make the most of this surprise?

EXCITEMENT

What specific event, opportunity, or idea is generating excitement for you?

What aspects of this situation resonate deeply with you?

EXCITEMENT

How can you channel this excitement into productive actions or pursuits?

What steps can you take to fully embrace and engage with this excitement?

JEALOUSY

What specifically triggers your jealousy?

How does this jealousy affect your self-perception?

JEALOUSY

What can you learn from the person or situation that triggers jealousy?

How can you shift from jealousy to gratitude and abundance?

What triggered your envy?

What qualities do you envy in others?

What need of yours is envy revealing?

How can you fulfill this need and find more satisfaction?

LOVE NOTE

A Love Note on Befriending Envy

Envy was an emotion that troubled me often, causing misery and discontentment. I would scroll through social media, comparing my life to others and feeling a sense of bitterness and annoyance. It was a never-ending cycle that left me feeling drained and unhappy.

I would see a picture of someone frolicking on a beautiful beach, looking perfect in a bright bikini, turquoise ocean sparking behind them. Meanwhile, I was hunched over my phone on the couch in raggedy sweatpants while a bitter-cold winter storm raged outside. The stark contrast fuelled my envy, and I would feel resentment toward this person who was sharing a moment of joy.

I would continue scrolling, fuelled by bitterness, seeking out the next person to dislike because their life seemed better than mine. It was an endless cycle of comparison and dissatisfaction. I felt trapped in a never-ending race to keep up with others, constantly feeling like I fell short.

But then, one day, a shift in perception occurred. I realized envy was not a negative emotion but rather a guide. It was trying to show me my unmet needs. This newfound understanding completely transformed my relationship with envy and how it felt in my body.

A few weeks later, I found myself scrolling through Instagram. It was still the dead of winter, and I had just finished leading an immersive teacher training weekend for our SAOR community. I was happy but exhausted, as these weekends required much of my energy to lead. I needed something, but I couldn't quite pinpoint what it was.

As I mindlessly scrolled, I saw a photo of someone on a vacation with their family. I didn't feel any envy. Instead, I felt a sense of contentment, and realized that my need to travel with my family had been fulfilled recently during a trip we had taken together. I genuinely felt joy for this person and their opportunity to experience quality time with their loved ones.

Continuing my scroll, I found a photo of a friend enjoying a retreat. Instantly, envy reared its head, and I recognized it as a sign of an unmet need within myself. I longed for time alone to recharge, learn, and grow in a direction solely my own. Instead of letting the envy consume me, I put my phone aside and shared my revelation with my husband.

We examined our calendar and found a block of time where our commitments were low. It was the perfect opportunity to invest in myself, to take the time and money to pursue personal growth and recharge. Acknowledging and addressing this unmet need, I took responsibility for my well-being and prevented depletion and despair.

Envy has become a catalyst for personal growth and self-care. It no longer holds power over me but serves as a reminder to acknowledge and address the unmet needs within myself. By shifting my perception and embracing envy as a guide, I have found a sense of joy and contentment that was once elusive. I am no longer haunted by envy but empowered by it, using it as a tool to navigate my journey toward fulfillment and happiness.

BOUNDARIES

“Just as we expect others to value our boundaries, it’s equally important for us to respect the boundaries of others.”

Laurie Buchanan, PhD

AWARENESS

ESTABLISHING AND UPHOLDING **HEALTHY BOUNDARIES**

Boundaries are guidelines that you set to protect yourself and maintain your well-being in various aspects of life. They are essential for personal growth, self-care, and establishing healthy relationships.

According to Dr. Nicole Lapera, a psychologist and author of How to Do the Work, setting boundaries that strike a balance between being too rigid and too loose is crucial for healthy functioning and fulfilling connections with others.

As you embark on a journey of self-improvement and prioritizing your well-being, it becomes essential to establish and uphold flexible boundaries. These boundaries protect your overall mental, emotional, and physical health. For example, as you strive to change old patterns, such as people-pleasing, you may encounter resistance from those who are accustomed to your previous behaviour.

To address this challenge, set flexible boundaries that allow your loved ones to understand the reasons behind your decision. By effectively communicating these boundaries, you can foster understanding and create healthier dynamics within your relationships. It is essential to recognize that boundaries are not negative or selfish, contrary to what society may have conditioned you to believe. Instead, they are powerful tools for self-respect, self-care, and asserting personal agency.

According to Dr. Nicole LaPera, there are three types of boundaries:

FLEXIBLE BOUNDARIES:

Individuals with flexible boundaries are open to giving and receiving in their relationships. They have a healthy balance between respecting their own needs and considering the needs of others. They can adapt to different situations and are generally comfortable with intimacy.

LOOSE BOUNDARIES:

People with loose boundaries have difficulty defining and maintaining healthy limits in their relationships. They may allow others to invade their personal space or exploit their generosity. They struggle to say "no" and often neglect their needs to please others. This can lead to feelings of overwhelm, resentment, and being taken advantage of.

RIGID BOUNDARIES:

Those with rigid boundaries have a strong need for control and distance in their relationships. They may avoid emotional intimacy and find it challenging to trust others. They have strict rules and limits, and it can be difficult to compromise or receive help from others. This can result in isolation and difficulties forming close connections.

Reflect on a time when you felt overwhelmed. What boundaries could have protected you?

How have boundaries positively impacted your relationships or interactions in the past?

Identify an area of your life where you currently have loose boundaries. How does this impact your well-being? What steps can you take to establish flexible boundaries in that area?

Explore an aspect of your life where you notice rigid boundaries. How might these boundaries be limiting your growth or connection with others?

Reflect on the benefits of setting boundaries for your overall self-care and mental health. How does practicing self-compassion and prioritizing your needs contribute to your well-being?

Dr. Nicole LePera states setting physical, emotional, and energetic boundaries is crucial for your well-being.

PHYSICAL BOUNDARIES:

Physical boundaries involve setting limits on how others can physically interact with you. They define your personal space, comfort levels, and physical needs. These boundaries ensure you feel safe, respected and have control over your body. By communicating and enforcing physical boundaries, you protect yourself from unwanted touch, invasion of personal space, or any physical discomfort.

EMOTIONAL BOUNDARIES:

Emotional boundaries are about recognizing and managing your feelings, needs, and desires separate from others. They help you maintain a sense of self and allow you to take responsibility for your emotions. By setting emotional boundaries, you avoid becoming overly enmeshed in the emotions of others, prevent emotional burnout, and maintain your emotional well-being.

ENERGETIC BOUNDARIES:

Energetic boundaries involve protecting and managing your energy levels and the energy you allow into your life. They help you preserve your vitality and mental wellbeing. By being aware of the people, situations, and environments that drain your energy or negatively impact you, you can set boundaries to limit your exposure to them. This allows you to maintain a positive and balanced state of mind.

PHYSICAL BOUNDARIES:

How do you feel when someone gets too close to you physically? How can you communicate this to others in a respectful way?

What are your comfort levels when it comes to physical touch? How can you establish and communicate these boundaries to ensure your comfort in social situations?

EMOTIONAL BOUNDARIES:

How do you differentiate between your own emotions and the emotions of others? How can you maintain a sense of self and take responsibility for your emotions?

Are there any relationships or situations where you tend to become overly involved with the emotions of others? How can you set boundaries to protect your emotional well-being?

ENERGETIC BOUNDARIES:

Reflect on situations or environments where you feel drained or overwhelmed. How can you set boundaries to limit your exposure to these energy-draining factors?

Are there any specific people in your life who deplete your energy? How can you establish limits and protect your energetic well-being around them?

Setting boundaries can be challenging, but a step-by-step action plan can make the process easier.

STEP 1

Identify your needs:

Take time to reflect on your feelings, values, and needs. Understand what is important to you and what you need to feel comfortable, safe, and respected in various areas of your life. This self-awareness is crucial in setting boundaries effectively.

STEP 2

Define your boundaries:

Once you clearly understand your needs, define your boundaries. Be specific about which behaviours, actions, or situations are acceptable or unacceptable. Consider different areas such as physical, emotional, and energetic boundaries.

STEP 3

Communicate assertively:

Once you've defined your boundaries, it's important to communicate them assertively to others. Choose an appropriate time and place to have a conversation. Use "I" statements to express how you feel and what you need, rather than blamingor criticizing the other person. Be clear, calm, and confident in your communication.

STEP 4

Set consequences:

Establish consequences for crossing or violating your boundaries. Consequences can vary depending on the situation and relationship, but they should be reasonable and enforceable. Communicate these consequences calmly and assertively, letting the other person know what will happen if they continue to disregard your boundaries.

STEP 5

Maintain consistency:

It's crucial to maintain consistency in enforcing your boundaries. This consistency helps others understand that your boundaries are not negotiable. Be firm in upholding your boundaries and following through with the consequences you've set.

STEP 6

Take responsibility for your emotions:

Recognize that you are responsible for your emotions and reactions. Setting boundaries can sometimes evoke negative responses from others, but remaining calm and assertive is essential.

STEP 7

Self-care and support:

Setting boundaries can be emotionally challenging, so it's important to prioritize self-care and seek support if needed. Practice self-compassion, engage in activities that recharge you, and reach out to trusted friends, family, or a therapist for guidance and encouragement.

STEP 8

Learn from experiences:

Reflect on your experiences and learn from them. Adjust and refine your boundaries, based on what works best for you and your relationships.

SUMMARY

Healthy boundaries are crucial for personal growth, self-care, and nourishing relationships. There are three types of boundaries: flexible, loose, and rigid. Flexible boundaries involve a healthy balance between one's own needs and the needs of others. In contrast, loose boundaries result in difficulties defining and maintaining healthy limits, often leading to feelings of overwhelm and being taken advantage of. Rigid boundaries involve a strong need for control and distance, resulting in isolation and difficulty forming close connections.

It is essential to establish and uphold flexible boundaries to protect overall well-being. This can be achieved through effective communication and recognizing that boundaries are tools for self respect and self-care. Setting boundaries involves reflecting on personal needs and values, defining them clearly, communicating assertively, maintaining consistency, practicing self-care, and seeking support when needed.

It may be challenging, but setting boundaries is an ongoing process that can lead to healthier and more-fulfilling connections with others. Use the action tool on the next page to establish your boundary and practice sharing it with someone you trust.

ACTION

COMMUNICATING HEALTHY BOUNDARIES

Using boundaries as a tool to communicate your needs is crucial because it helps you maintain healthy relationships, prevent resentment, and foster mutual respect. It establishes a clear framework of what you find acceptable and helps others understand how their actions impact you. Boundaries create a foundation for open and honest communication, where both parties can understand and consider each other's needs. By effectively using boundaries, you can maintain healthier and more fulfilling connections with the people around you.

Identify the boundary you wish to establish: Clearly define the behaviour, action, or situation you want to address.

Reflect on your needs and feelings: Take a moment to understand how this boundary violation affects you. Identify the emotions, thoughts, and needs that arise when this boundary is crossed.

Use the following script as a guide, adapting it to your specific situation:

Sample Script:

Hi [person's name],

I wanted to talk to you about something that has been on my mind and affecting our relationship. I value your connection, and I believe open communication is essential.

Recently, I've noticed [describe the specific behaviour or situation that violates your boundary]. It's important for me to express how this behaviour makes me feel and establish a boundary you can both respect.

When [describe the behaviour], I feel [share your emotions, thoughts, and needs related to this boundary violation]. I must have [state the specific boundary you want to establish] to maintain a healthy relationship and care for my well-being.

I hope you understand where I'm coming from and respect this boundary. I believe we can strengthen our relationship and ensure mutual respect by communicating openly and honestly.

Thank you for listening, and I appreciate your support in honouring this boundary.

Sincerely,
[your namc]

Remember, this script is just a guide. Feel free to modify it according to your needs and the nature of your relationship with the person involved. Practice expressing your boundaries assertively and with compassion, valuing your well-being and fostering healthy connections.

Define your boundary: Clearly and precisely articulate the boundary you want to establish. Use "I" statements to express how their behaviour affects you.

LOVE NOTE

A Love Note on Rebuilding Trust

I have always been aware of my mistrust pattern. I don't know where it originated, but I am conscious of the moments that fueled it. As a small girl in elementary school, I was bullied regularly. In high school, I was victimized by "mean girls." And I was cheated on in a long-term relationship. I didn't have many meaningful relationships because even a hint of conflict would make me run for the hills. By the time I met my husband, I was not a trusting person.

When Mark and I first got together, I tried to break up with him multiple times. Fortunately, he had the courage to make me work through our conflicts together. This was the first time I witnessed the power of conflict as a way to strengthen and build meaningful connections. As our relationship deepened, we built trust that provided me with a safe space to explore my trust issues more deeply.

By the time we got married, had two children, and were settling into a life together, I realized I had formed an unhealthy, anxious attachment to my husband. Whenever he went out with friends, I worried he would get hit by a drunk driver or worse. When he travelled on trips with his friends, I couldn't sleep and would have paralyzing anxiety, fearing that he would meet another woman and have an affair. My anxiety became so overwhelming that my husband lost all desire to go out with friends or travel for fun. He worried about my mental health and didn't want to disrupt the peace I felt when he was home safe with me. It was at this point I realized I needed to take responsibility for my pattern of mistrust.

I met with my therapist and shared how despite my husband being a loyal and safe individual, I regularly had paranoid thoughts that he would leave me for another woman or be harmed. These thoughts were utterly unfounded and deeply irrational, yet they felt so real in my body.

Over many months, my therapist helped me see how my past experiences created a mistrust pattern. She guided me in communicating to my husband how these experiences had shaped my automatic thought process, how those thoughts made me feel (desperate and alone), and how I could set healthy and flexible boundaries to protect my mental health and Mark's independence.

These boundaries allowed my husband to be his own person without worrying that he would hurt me. Whenever he went out, knowing that I was at home worrying, he would text me at various points in the evening to let me know when he was safe and when he was coming home. He would return at a reasonable hour, understanding that I couldn't fall asleep without him home safe beside me. With these new boundaries in place, I was able to remain calm. I continued to work with my therapist and began healing some parts of me that were triggering the pattern. With time, my husband could go out and even travel without me being triggered. My anxiety had completely subsided, and I felt like my rational self again.

I put all my new tools in place on a recent trip to Mexico. Our entire family went to cheer my husband on at an Ironman event. I noticed a couple of women in our hotel, who were also participating in the Ironman, chatting with my husband regularly about the race. I would have become jealous and gotten angry at my husband in the past, but I kept my cool this time. After the race, I noticed my husband commiserating with the women in the lobby about how difficult the race was. One of them had had too much to drink and became flirtatious with Mark. My husband wasn't encouraging the flirtation, but he seemed oblivious to how it made me feel. I was furious. All my old patterns were triggered, and I reverted to that defenceless little girl who felt abandoned all those years ago. My mind was filled with irrational thoughts as I argued with him in my head. I couldn't believe he was allowing them to flirt with him. It felt disrespectful to me, and I started to believe they were more attractive to him than me. I worried that he would leave me for them. These irrational thoughts consumed me throughout the night, causing me to lose sleep and spiral deeper into my negative emotions.

The next day, I tried to remember the tools my therapist had taught me. I listened to a grounding meditation and took time to journal about the situation and what I needed. It may have seemed trivial, but what I needed most was reassurance. I needed to hear that those women were insignificant to him, that my husband loved me and wasn't going anywhere. When I shared this with him, he was more than happy to provide the reassurance I needed and my mood improved. By openly communicating my needs, I established new boundaries to protect my mental health and well-being in that situation.

I had to learn that my feelings are not wrong and that boundaries are a communication tool that help me express my needs. Boundaries are flexible and evolve as I heal and grow. I encourage you to explore your needs based on your lived experiences and communicate those needs to those you want to share a life with. Sharing boundaries is not negative; it's a way to create healthier and more fulfilling relationships.

the NERVOUS SYSTEM

Andrew Taylor Still

AWARENESS

UNDERSTANDING THE HARMONIOUS DANCE OF YOUR **NERVOUS SYSTEM**

The autonomic nervous system is a complex network of nerves that controls your body's involuntary functions. It acts as a communication system between your brain and your body, helping to regulate essential bodily processes without conscious effort. The anatomic nervous system is divided into two branches: the sympathetic and parasympathetic nervous systems.

The sympathetic nervous system is responsible for the "fight or flight" response. It prepares the body for action during times of perceived threat or stress. It increases heart rate, elevates blood pressure, dilates the pupils, and diverts blood flow to the muscles and lungs, enabling you to respond quickly to potential dangers.

On the other hand, the parasympathetic nervous system is responsible for the "rest and digest" response. It helps conserve energy and promotes relaxation. It slows your heart rate, lowers blood pressure, stimulates digestion, and promotes healing and repair processes in the body.

It is important to balance the two systems because they play complementary roles in maintaining your overall well-being. While the sympathetic nervous system prepares you for action, it can be taxing if constantly activated, leading to chronic stress-related health issues. Conversely, an overactive parasympathetic system may result in sluggishness and reduced alertness.

Improving your ability to shift between the sympathetic and parasympathetic nervous systems when appropriate is essential to maintaining optimal health. For instance, during times of stress or urgency, activating the sympathetic system can be beneficial. However, after the stressful event has passed, it's important to engage the parasympathetic system to promote relaxation, recovery, and overall balance.

Finding ways to shift between these two systems can be achieved through techniques like breathing exercises, mindfulness, physical activity, spending time in nature, engaging in hobbies, and cultivating positive relationships. By being aware of your body's signals and practicing selfcare, you can ensure that both the sympathetic and parasympathetic systems are utilized appropriately, leading to a healthier and more balanced life.

When the nervous system becomes dysregulated, one or both branches of the anatomic nervous system are not functioning optimally.

In a dysregulated sympathetic state, the sympathetic nervous system is excessively activated, leading to symptoms such as heightened anxiety, increased heart rate, muscle tension, exhaustion and a constant state of alertness.

On the other hand, a dysregulated parasympathetic state indicates an underactivation of the parasympathetic nervous system, which can result in symptoms such as fatigue, brain fog, digestive issues, and difficulty concentrating.

It is important to emphasize that multiple factors, such as chronic stress, trauma, lifestyle habits, and underlying health conditions, can potentially impact nervous system dysregulation. Therefore, seeking professional support is strongly recommended in such circumstances.

Here are some symptoms that may indicate a dysregulated state in each branch:

DYSREGULATED SYMPATHETIC NERVOUS STATE:

- Increased heart rate and palpitations
- Elevated blood pressure
- Rapid, shallow breathing or hyperventilation
- Excessive sweating
- Heightened anxiety or panic attacks
- Increased muscle tension and restlessness
- Digestive issues like stomach aches
- Insomnia or difficulties in falling asleep

DYSREGULATED PARASYMPATHETIC NERVOUS STATE:

- Sluggishness and fatigue
- Low heart rate and blood pressure
- Digestive issues such as constipation
- Excessive drowsiness or feeling lethargic
- Poor concentration and mental fog
- Decreased motivation or lack of interest
- Excessive tearfulness or emotional sensitivity
- Cold hands and feet

It's important to note that these symptoms can vary among individuals. Recognizing these signs is important for understanding when your nervous system may be out of balance and taking steps to restore equilibrium, which you will explore next.

If you notice persistent or severe symptoms of dysregulation, it is always advisable to consult with a healthcare professional for proper evaluation and guidance on managing your specific situation.

How do you generally feel throughout the day? Are there noticeable fluctuations in your energy levels, mood, or physical sensations?

Describe any physical symptoms you experience regularly. Do any of your symptoms appear in the dysregulated state chart you just reviewed?

Pay attention to your body's response to stress. How quickly does your heart rate increase? Do you tend to hold tension in specific muscles or experience digestive issues during stress?

Reflect on your breathing patterns. Shallow breaths may indicate a sympathetic response, whereas longer, slower breaths may suggest a parasympathetic nervous state.

How do you respond to self-care practices? Are you able to engage in activities that bring you joy and relaxation? Do you struggle with allowing yourself to rest or prioritize your well-being?

Reflect on any past experiences or significant life events that may have contributed to your current state. How have these experiences impacted your nervous system and overall well-being?

SUMMARY

Maintaining a balance between the sympathetic and parasympathetic nervous systems is imperative for overall well-being. The sympathetic system prepares the body for action, while the parasympathetic system induces relaxation. Too much activation of the sympathetic nervous system can result in stress-related health problems, while an overactive parasympathetic nervous system can cause sluggishness and reduced alertness. Recognizing symptoms of a dysregulated nervous system is vital to understanding when the balance is disrupted.

By incorporating regular self-care techniques and tools discussed in the following section, you can greatly enhance the well-being of your anatomical nervous system, ultimately paving the way for a more radiant and healthy life.

ACTIVATE YOUR VAGUS NERVE

The vagus nerve is the longest cranial nerve in your body and is vital in regulating various bodily functions. It connects your brain to many organs, including the heart, lungs, digestive, and immune systems. Stimulating the vagus nerve can help reduce stress, promote relaxation, improve digestion, enhance mood, and even boost your immune system. By activating the vagus nerve, you can regulate your nervous system and restore a sense of inner balance.

An audio version is available at www.insighttimer.com/saorstudio.

Stimulate your vagus nerve to calm your body.

Find a quiet place where you can lie down comfortably. Close your eyes, and take a few slow breaths in and out of your body. Give yourself permission to rest here for a moment. Notice as your body softens, your thoughts gradually follow a gentler rhythm.

Bring your attention to your breath. Take a slow, deep inhale through your nose, allowing your belly to rise. Then, exhale gently through your mouth, letting your belly fall. Continue this slow, deep breathing pattern throughout the meditation.

Now, imagine a soft, warm light glowing in the center of your chest, where your heart is. Visualize this light expanding and radiating throughout your entire body, continuing your efforts to soothe and relax every part of you.

As you continue breathing, allow the light to fade away and bring your focus to the area around the crown of your head. Imagine gentle waves of relaxation flowing from your crown into your chest, belly, arms and legs. Feel these waves of peace spreading throughout your body, releasing tension or stress.

Next, shift your attention to your belly. Place one hand on your stomach and take a moment to feel the warmth of your hand where it rests. Place the other hand on your heart and take a moment to feel the gentleness of your own embrace. As you breathe, visualize the breath carrying your love, reaching every part of you.

Repeat silently, "I am calm, centered, and content. My body and mind are in harmony."

Allow yourself to stay relaxed for a few more minutes, enjoying the sensations of rest and tranquility. If distracting thoughts arise, acknowledge them and let them pass without judgment, gently bringing your focus back to your breath, body and touch.

When you feel ready, slowly open your eyes and take a moment to reorient yourself to your surroundings. Notice how you feel. It's beneficial to make a mindful effort like this one a regular practice to experience the long-term benefits of vagus-nerve stimulation fully.

ACTION

DISCOVER THE POWER OF BREATH

This deep-breathing exercise is a powerful tool for activating the relaxation response, slowing down your heart rate, and fostering a deep sense of balance in your nervous system. It can be practiced whenever you feel overwhelmed or need to regulate your nervous system.

An audio version is available at www.insighttimer.com/saorstudio.

Pause and breath intentionally to restore peace and calm.

To begin, find a comfortable place to sit or lie down. Close your eyes, take a moment to settle in, and fully embrace this moment unfolding for you. Scan your body and release any tension that may feel heavy or unwelcome.

Place one hand on your belly and the other on your chest. As you take a slow, deep breath in through your nose, feel the hand on your belly rise while keeping your chest relatively still. Allow yourself to pause momentarily at the top of your breath, fully taking in the nourishing air available.

Exhale slowly and steadily through your nose, allowing your belly to fall as you release the air. Pay attention to the feeling of your stomach lowering, while keeping your chest motionless. Pause again at the bottom of your breath, savouring the moment of stillness and release.

Continue this deep-breathing cycle for a few moments to establish a relaxed and steady rhythm. With each breath, consciously release any tension or stress, envisioning it as unnecessary energy leaving your body.

As you breathe deeply, gradually bring your focus back to your surroundings. When you feel ready, gently open your eyes. Allow yourself to bask in the sense of peace this exercise promotes in your body.

Regular practice of this deep-breathing exercise can provide immense benefits for your overall well-being and help you navigate the challenges of daily life with a greater sense of calm and equilibrium.

ALTERNATE NOSTRIL BREATHING FOR BALANCE AND CLARITY

Alternate nostril breathing, also known as Nadi Shodhana or Anulom Vilom, is a breathing technique originating from ancient yogic traditions in India. This practice involves alternating the breath between the left and right nostrils, which is believed to have numerous benefits for physical and mental well-being. This practice helps balance the nervous system, reducing stress and anxiety by promoting a state of calm and relaxation. It also improves focus and concentration by enhancing mental clarity and balancing the brain's energy flow.

An audio version is available at www.insighttimer.com/saorstudio.

Create deeper clarity with focused breathwork.

Find a comfortable seated position with your spine straight and shoulders relaxed.

Rest your left hand on your left knee, palm facing upward or downward—whatever feels comfortable.

Bring your right hand up to your face and lightly place the tips of your index and middle fingers between your eyebrows. Your ring finger can rest on your left nostril and your thumb on your right nostril.

Close your right nostril with your thumb and inhale slowly and deeply through your left nostril. Fill your lungs completely.

At the top of the inhalation, release your right nostril and close your left nostril with your ring finger. Exhale fully and slowly through your right nostril.

Inhale deeply through your right nostril, then close it with your thumb. Release your left nostril and exhale through it.

Continue this alternate nostril breathing pattern, exhaling and inhaling through one nostril, switching, and exhaling and inhaling through the other nostril. Each breath should be slow, deep, and controlled. Aim to practice for about five minutes, gradually increasing the duration as you become more comfortable with the technique.

Remember to breathe naturally and without force. Focus on the sensation of the breath as it enters and leaves your nostrils. With regular practice, alternate nostril breathing can become a valuable tool for relaxation, mental clarity, and overall well-being.

It's important to note that controlled breathwork may not be suitable for everyone. If you feel lightheaded or uncomfortable at any point, please discontinue the practice and consult a healthcare professional if necessary.

RENEWED VITALITY WITH BREATH OF FIRE

When stuck in the parasympathetic state, your body and mind operate more slowly. While important for relaxation, staying in this space too long can hinder your ability to respond effectively to challenges or feel productive. Breath of Fire can help you activate the sympathetic nervous system, boosting alertness and energy levels, and help improve stress-coping mechanisms. This increases engagement, productivity, and adaptability, leading to a more balanced and fulfilling life.
Breath of Fire is commonly done as part of Kundalini Yoga and is known for its energizing and purifying effects. It can increase vitality, clear the mind, and activate energy centers.

An audio version is available at www.insighttimer.com/saorstudio.

Recharge and fire up your energy source.

Close your eyes if you're comfortable doing so, and take a few deep breaths to center yourself.

Start by inhaling deeply through your nose, filling your lungs about halfway.

Exhale with force and speed through your mouth, pushing the air out in rapid bursts. The sound produced should resemble a "ha" or "huh." Use the strength of your abdominal muscles to expel the air more forcefully than during a regular breath.

Continue this quick and forceful exhale, followed by a passive inhale through your nose. The inhale should happen naturally as a reflex to the exhale, without conscious effort.

As you get comfortable with the rhythm, try to increase the speed of your breath, making it as quick and powerful as possible while maintaining control. Keep the breath rhythmic and continuous, creating a steady flow of rapid exhales and passive inhales.

Start with a duration of thirty seconds and gradually work your way up to three minutes or longer if you feel comfortable.

Throughout the exercise, focus on the sensation of the breath moving in and out of your nostrils. After completing the desired duration, take a deep breath in and exhale slowly, allowing your breath to return to its natural rhythm.

Take a moment to observe the effects of the breath exercise on your energy levels and overall state of mind.

Open your eyes, stretch your body if needed, and carry the energizing effects with you throughout your day.

It's important to note that the Breath of Fire may not be suitable for everyone, especially if you have respiratory or cardiovascular issues. If you feel lightheaded or uncomfortable at any point, please discontinue the practice and consult a healthcare professional if necessary.

UNRAVEL TENSION WITH PROGRESSIVE MUSCLE RELAXATION

Progressive Muscle Relaxation is a technique that involves gently tensing and then relaxing different muscle groups in your body. This practice can be helpful in relieving stress, reducing muscle tension, and promoting overall relaxation. By focusing on your body and allowing it to unwind, you also create the perfect environment for your mind to let go.

An audio version is available at www.insighttimer.com/saorstudio.

Find deeper relaxation with this mindful exercise.

To begin, find a quiet, cozy space to either sit or lie down. Make any necessary modifications to ensure that your position is comfortable. Close your eyes and take a few deep breaths, allowing your mind and body to begin relaxing. As you settle into a state of calmness, start by directing your attention toward your breath, allowing it to become slow and steady.

Draw your focus to your hands. Begin by clenching your fists tightly, feeling tension in your hands and forearms. Hold this tension for a few seconds, then release, letting your hands and arms go limp. As you do so, notice the contrast between the earlier tension and the present relaxation spreading through your muscles. Take a moment to feel gratitude for this release.

Now, shift your attention to your arms. Tense your upper arms by flexing your muscles, feeling the tightness and tension building up. Hold this tension for a few seconds, then release it, allowing the tension to melt away. Feel your muscles becoming loose and relaxed as if they are gently unraveling.

Shift your focus to your face. Scrunch up your face, wrinkle your nose, squeeze your eyes shut, and clench your jaw. Feel the tension in your facial muscles. Hold this tension for a few seconds, then release it, letting all the strain fade. Allow your face to soften, and feel the relaxation spreading throughout every muscle.

Next, bring your attention to your chest and stomach. Take in a deep inhale, pull your abdominal muscles towards your spine, pull your bottom ribs towards your hip bones, squeeze and hold it for a few seconds, then exhale slowly, allowing your belly and chest to relax completely. Feel the weight of tension releasing from your torso, and notice the gentle rhythm of your breath as it brings you deeper into a state of rest.

Now, shift your focus to your back. Arch your back slightly and draw your shoulder blades together, feeling the tension build in your lower and upper back. Hold this position for a few seconds, then release, allowing your spine and shoulder blades to relax. Feel any strain or tightness melting away, leaving you with a sense of ease and comfort.

Moving down to your thighs, tense your thigh muscles by pressing your legs together and locking your knee joints. Reach your heels forward, hold this tension for a few seconds, and then release, letting your legs go limp. Feel the heaviness leaving your thighs as they become completely relaxed and rotate outwards.

Bring your attention to your calves. Flex your ankles, reaching your toes toward your shins and your heels away from you. Hold this position for a few seconds, then release it, allowing your calves to relax. Feel the tension dissipating as your muscles become loose and at ease.

Finally, direct your attention to your feet and toes. Curl your toes tightly, feeling the tension in your feet. Hold this tension for a few seconds, then release it, letting your feet and toes completely relax. Notice the sensation of relaxation spreading through your feet as any remaining tightness is released.

Take a few moments to enjoy the feeling of relaxation in your entire body. Allow yourself to embrace this state of calmness and peace. Feel the soothing energy flow freely through your muscles, creating a sense of tranquility within.

When you're ready, slowly open your eyes and bring your awareness back to your surroundings. Take a moment to appreciate the effort you've put into this practice and its positive impact on your mind and body. Be mindful that you are thinking grateful thoughts and pausing to feel the sensation of gratitude in your body as well.

Progressive Muscle Relaxation can be adjusted to suit your needs. Feel free to spend more time on particularly tense or tight areas. With regular practice, you'll develop a deeper connection with your body and an increased ability to release tension and stress when you need it most.

LOVE NOTE

A Love Note on Rising Above the Flood

Sundays are usually a chance to unwind and indulge in restful activities. However, a particular Sunday in April 2022 deviated from the usual norm. I had lead an intense 20-hour SAOR Teacher Training module spanning across Friday and Saturday. As Sunday morning arrived, I found myself utterly exhausted, both physically and mentally, after the relentless activity and exertion.

I felt a strange urge to check in on the studio that afternoon. However, as the day progressed, my motivation to go to the studio dwindled. Instead, I shifted my focus to spending quality time with my family.

In the evening, just as my husband and I were enjoying a rare dinner alone, I received a text from Sylvia. She simply asked me to give her a call. My heart sank, and I knew something was wrong. Without hesitation, I dialed her number, and she informed me that one of our trainers had arrived at the studio to prepare for the evening class, only to find a significant amount of water on the floor. Sylvia was on her way to assess the situation, but it seemed likely that we would have to cancel the class that evening.

My husband and I quickly packed up our meal to eat later and hurried over to the studio to assess the damage. Luckily, our children were happily occupied with friends who kindly offered to look after them for a bit longer while we dealt with the situation. Initially, we believed we would only be gone for an hour, but we were mistaken.

Upon arrival, we discovered a few members of our team frantically attempting to remove water from the reception area and studios. It turned out that earlier in the day, while the studio was empty, the hose on our filtered water fountain had come loose, causing water to flood the studio. Imagine leaving a garden hose running in your home for six hours with nowhere for the water to drain. Although it was clean, filtered water, the damage had already been done. I couldn't help but wonder how different things would have been if I had followed my intuition and gone into the studio that afternoon. So much of the mess could have been avoided.

Without hesitation, I contacted my landlord, who also owned a dental clinic below the studio. I was concerned about water seeping downwards due to the laws of gravity. Then, I shifted into "fight mode," channeling all my energy into mitigating the damage and protecting our newly constructed studio floors. Despite the chaos, I still felt a sense of control and optimism that we could contain the situation.

Just as we were finishing up and I felt my nervous system begin to stabilize, I received a text from my landlord. She included photos of her office, and the damage was devastating. It resembled the aftermath of a tropical storm sweeping through one side of her clinic. Once again, I sprang into action, gathering mops, towels, and the Shop-Vac, and headed downstairs with Mark and Sylvia to assist in cleaning up the dental clinic while the others wrapped up work in our studio.

At that moment, the weight of the situation hit me fully. I understood how much effort my landlord had put into creating a safe and beautiful space for children in her dental clinic. Witnessing the flood damage to her dream shattered my heart. I called a friend and asked if she could find a sitter to pick up my kids and put them to bed because it was clear we wouldn't be home anytime soon. My friend graciously agreed, and we devoted all our energy to helping salvage whatever we could from the dental clinic.

For several hours, we labored tirelessly, mopping up water, moving furniture, and attempting to dry out the space as much as possible. It felt like an overwhelming task, but the sense of camaraderie among us kept me going. We supported and encouraged one another, shared stories, and even managed to find moments of levity amidst the devastation.

Finally, the water was fully cleaned up, and we assessed the remaining damage. The floors would require drying and restoration, some furniture would need replacement, and repairs had to be made to the walls and ceilings. It was clear that we had a long road ahead, but at least the immediate crisis was over.

In the following days, we worked tirelessly to bring everything back to normal. Contractors were called in, repairs were scheduled, and insurance claims were filed. It was a whirlwind of phone calls, meetings, and paperwork, but we remained determined to overcome this challenging situation.

Throughout this trying time, I found myself fluctuating between various nervous states that manifested as anxiety and fear in my body. There were moments when I felt scared, anxious, and overwhelmed with the thought of potential setbacks. What if the insurance didn't cover the damage? What if we couldn't reopen? After being shut down due to the pandemic for nearly two years and only just reopening, my nervous system was already on edge, and I wasn't sure if I could handle another blow. When these fearful thoughts clouded my judgment, I knew it was crucial to pause, step back, and find balance within my nervous system. Deep breathing, self-care rituals, and allowing myself to receive support from others became the tools I relied on to regulate my nervous system whenever I felt symptoms of dysregulation creeping in.

The support from our SAOR community during this time was truly incredible. Community members and our team rallied together, offering their help, support, and encouragement. It served as a humbling reminder of the strength and resilience that can be found within a close-knit community.

Reflecting on that fateful Sunday, I can't help but feel a deep sense of appreciation. I am grateful for the unwavering support of our community, the determination and resilience of our team, and the valuable lessons learned. It served as a reminder that even in the face of adversity, we can come together, overcome challenges, and emerge stronger than before. Without my ability to regulate my nervous system, I'm not sure if I would have been able to open myself up to receive the abundance of support that was available to me.

MINDFULNESS

"In today's rush, we all think too much, seek too much, want too much, and forget about the joy of just being."

Eckhart Tolle

AWARENESS

UNLEASH THE **POWER OF MINDFULNESS**

Embracing mindfulness in your daily life involves slowing down and becoming more aware of your choices. You may have been conditioned to believe that constantly achieving, doing, and being in perpetual motion is the sole path to success. However, based on my personal experiences, adopting this lifestyle has only led to heightened levels of anxiety, exhaustion, and burnout. It wasn't until I discovered the value of integrating mindfulness into my pursuit of achievement that I truly grasped my potential for success in various aspects of life, including my relationships, parenting, and career.

Cultivating regular mindful practices in your life is important because it enables you to nurture and grow this ability. What you intentionally practice, you strengthen. Remember, when you embark on something new, you might initially feel like a beginner and lack proficiency. Mindfulness is like riding a bike for the first time – it may not feel natural at first, but persevere, and soon enough, you will excel.

Here are some of the many benefits you can achieve with a consistent mindfulness practice:

PRESENT MOMENT AWARENESS:

Mindfulness cultivates the ability to be fully present in the current moment. It shifts your attention away from worries about the past or future, allowing you to appreciate and engage with the here and now. By being present, you can experience life more fully and deeply.

REDUCED STRESS AND ANXIETY:

Mindfulness has been shown to reduce stress and anxiety levels. When you are mindful, you observe your thoughts and emotions without judgment or attachment. This non-reactive and accepting attitude helps to break the cycle of stress, promoting a greater sense of calm.

IMPROVED MENTAL HEALTH:

A regular mindfulness practice can enhance your overall emotional resilience, self-awareness, and self-compassion. Mindfulness helps you develop a healthier relationship with your thoughts and emotions, leading to greater emotional balance and positive mental states.

BETTER DECISION-MAKING:

When you are mindful, you become aware of your automatic patterns of thinking and reacting, allowing you to respond to situations with greater clarity and wisdom. This can lead to better decision-making and problem-solving abilities.

INCREASED PHYSICAL HEALTH:

Mindfulness practices can help reduce blood pressure, improve sleep quality, boost the immune system, and decrease chronic pain symptoms. Mindfulness positively impacts your overall physical well-being by reducing stress and promoting relaxation.

SELF-DISCOVERY:

Mindfulness practice encourages self-reflection and self-discovery. Observing your thoughts, emotions, and behaviour patterns gives you insight into yourself and your inner workings.

REFLECT ON YOUR DAILY ROUTINE

Take a few moments to write down your typical daily routine. Identify any areas where you feel rushed, stressed, or disconnected. How can you bring mindfulness and presence into these specific moments? Write down actionable steps you can take to be more present.

ASSESS YOUR EMOTIONAL WELL-BEING

Reflect on your emotional state throughout the day. Are there particular situations or triggers that lead to negative emotions or stress? Journal about these triggers and consider how you can bring more mindfulness to these moments.

RELATIONSHIPS AND COMMUNICATION

Consider your relationships with loved ones, friends, or colleagues. Reflect on how you can be more present and attentive during conversations, practice active listening, and respond with empathy and understanding.

MINDFUL SELF-CARE

Are there any areas where you need to pay more attention to self-care or engage in mindful activities? Journal about the activities or practices that nourish and rejuvenate you. Consider setting aside dedicated time for self-care and explore mindful practices such as meditation, yoga and breathwork.

IDENTIFYING LIFE VALUES

Reflect on your core values and what truly matters. Consider how aligned your current rituals and choices are with those values. Write down specific steps you can take to live more in alignment with your values and make choices that reflect them.

SUMMARY

By intentionally slowing down and becoming more aware of your choices, you can experience life more fully and deeply. Through consistent mindfulness practice, you can nurture and strengthen your ability to be fully present, observe your thoughts and emotions without judgment, and make conscious and deliberate choices. Mindfulness allows you to live with greater awareness, compassion, intention, and resilience, ultimately leading to a more fulfilling and balanced life.

By regularly practicing the mindfulness tools provided in the following section, you can effectively reap the rewards of mindfulness, improving relaxation and sharpening focus.

MINDFUL OF YOUR NEEDS

How often do you pause and intentionally direct your focus to the present moment and recognize your needs before they are neglected? As a mother and entrepreneur, my schedule is filled with responsibilities and demands to support others. However, when I take a moment to practice mindfulness, I give myself the chance to slow down and reconnect with my own desires. By responding to my needs first, I can maintain my resilience and energy levels, enabling me to continue supporting others in a meaningful way.

An audio version is available at www.insighttimer.com/saorstudio.

Pause and take time to meet your needs.

Shift your focus to the present moment, noticing any sounds, sensations, or thoughts that arise. Instead of pushing them away, observe them without judgment and let them come and go effortlessly. Turn your attention to your breath. Feel the natural rhythm of your inhale and exhale, the sensation of air entering and leaving your body. Continue to follow the breath without trying to control it.

While you continue to breathe, pay attention to any areas of tension or discomfort in your body. Send your breath to those areas, allowing them to soften as you release the tension, creating space for stillness and a sense of ease.

Let your breath be your anchor, grounding you in the present moment. If your mind wanders, gently guide it back to your breath as a point of focus and stability.

Expand your awareness to your surroundings. Notice sensations like the fabric of your clothes on your skin, the temperature in the room, and hairs on the back of your neck. Embrace all the sensations available to you at this moment.

Stay present and bring to mind a place that brings you peace. Picture this special space in your mind's eye and feel gratitude for it in your heart. Envision yourself in this safe and serene place. See yourself enjoying this space with an open heart, and acknowledge your worth and goodness. Offer words of love and acceptance to yourself, affirming your well-being.

Take a few moments to rest in this space of awareness and compassion. Observe any sensations or emotions that arise without judgment or attachment. Ask yourself, "What do I need in this moment?" and listen with an open heart. Give yourself space to hear the answer without the urgency to respond. Be open to creating awareness for your own needs.

Wiggle your fingers and toes, stretch if you desire, and slowly open your eyes. Carry the sense of calmness and well-being with you. Consider any needs that surfaced during the meditation and think of something small you can do today to fulfill one of them. Trust in your ability to create space for yourself and meet your needs.

Remember, this is a practice; it is okay if your mind wanders or you feel resistance. Be patient and gentle with yourself, knowing that each moment of mindfulness contributes to regulating your nervous system.

ACTION

CULTIVATE PRESENT-MOMENT AWARENESS

The five senses meditation is a mindfulness practice that involves bringing awareness to each of your senses, one at a time, to cultivate present-moment awareness. It helps ground you in the here and now. It enhances sensory perception, allowing you to fully experience and appreciate your environment's richness. This practice also promotes a sense of calm, reduces anxiety, and fosters a greater connection with your body and surroundings.

An audio version is available at www.insighttimer.com/saorstudio.

Pause and pull yourself into this moment.

See: Start by gently closing your eyes and bringing your attention to your sense of sight. Notice any colours, patterns, or shapes you see behind your closed eyelids. Observe without judgment, simply being aware of the visual sensations. Take note of the obvious visuals and then redirect your attention towards the less noticeable sights that had previously escaped your initial awareness.

Hear: Shift your focus to your sense of hearing. Tune in to the sounds around you, both near and far. Notice any subtle sounds or even the silence between sounds. Pay attention to the quality and texture of each sound without getting caught up in thoughts or judgments.

Smell: Bring your attention to your sense of smell. Notice any aromas or scents in your environment. It could be the smell of a nearby plant, food, or even the freshness of the air. Allow yourself to fully experience each scent as you inhale, without analyzing or attaching any particular meaning. Allow curiosity to be your guide as you experience these smells.

Taste: Now, shift your focus to your sense of taste. Notice any lingering taste in your mouth or any sensations on your tongue. It could be sweetness, bitterness, or a neutral taste. Observe the sensations without engaging in thought.

Feel: Lastly, bring your attention to your sense of touch. Notice the feeling of your body against the surface you're sitting or lying on. Pay attention to any sensations on your skin, such as warmth, coolness, or the feeling of clothing against your body. Are there any internal sensations you notice, like your heart beating or cells transforming? Observe the sensations without reacting or trying to change them.

Now, take a moment to combine all of your five senses and become aware of what you see, hear, smell, taste, and feel all at once. Observe without judgment and try not to create a story around your experience. Once you feel satisfied with this observation, shift your focus back to your breath and take three slow, deep breaths in and out, allowing yourself to let go of your senses for now and be fully present in this current moment. Direct your awareness to the space in the middle of your forehead and inquire within by asking yourself, "What is the message I need to hear right now?" Open yourself up to hearing your inner voice and uncover the guidance you seek.

ACTION

FEEL CALM AND CONTENT

One of the most wonderful aspects of meditation is its ability to leave you feeling calm and content. It is a powerful practice that can help you find peace and serenity amidst the chaos of life. It is a powerful practice that can help us find peace and serenity amidst the chaos of life. With this in mind, I have created a guided visualization that aims to assist you in achieving this desired state of tranquillity and inner peace. This visualization is particularly beneficial during moments when you find yourself overwhelmed or drained, as it serves as a gentle reminder to take a step back and reconnect with your inner self. Allow yourself to tap into a deep sense of relaxation and rejuvenation, giving your mind and body an opportunity to rest and recharge.

An audio version is available at www.insighttimer.com/saorstudio.

Permission to slow down and feel calm and content.

Find a quiet spot where you can relax without any interruptions. Lie in a comfortable position and soften your gaze, or if it's comfortable, close your eyes. Take a few calming breaths, inhaling through your nose and exhaling through your mouth, allowing your body to relax with each breath. From the top of your head to the tips of your toes, feel yourself gradually sinking deeper into this present moment.

Imagine yourself standing in a serene natural setting, surrounded by enchanting beauty. Picture vivid hues of greens, blues, and yellows, as though encountering these colours for the very first time. Inhale deeply, letting the scents of blooming flowers and earthy freshness permeate your being, awakening every sense within you. As you breathe, sense a gentle breeze caressing your skin, offering a soothing touch that relaxes your muscles and puts your body at ease.

As you continue to breathe slowly, imagine that each inhale offers you a sense of calmness. With each exhale, release any tension, stress, or negativity from your body and mind, leaving you feeling content.

While standing in this calming and inviting space, focus on the sounds around you. Listen to the soothing chirping of birds or the gentle rustling of leaves in the wind. Perhaps you hear the babble of a brook nearby or ocean waves rolling up on the sandy shore. Let these sounds deepen your contentment even further.

Now, envision a comfortable chair placed within this safe space. Imagine yourself sitting in this chair, feeling fully supported and at ease. As you sit, allow yourself to fully embrace the present moment, experiencing a profound sense of calmness and contentment.

Take a few moments to simply be present in this serene space, embracing the calmness within you. Notice your ability to slow down as you exist at this moment. Give yourself permission to linger a little longer than you intended. Staying with your breath. Staying with yourself. Calm and content.

When you feel ready, slowly bring your awareness back to the present moment. Gently wiggle your fingers and toes, stretch your body, and open your eyes.

Take a moment to reflect on the feelings you experienced during this guided visualization. Allow your awareness to boost your confidence in your ability to recreate this sensation anytime and anywhere you desire.

BOX BREATH FOR STRESS AND ANXIETY RELIEF

Box Breath meditation is a simple and effective technique that promotes a sense of calm and relaxation. This technique involves equal-length inhales, holds, exhales, and holds. It was first recommended to me by my therapist and has been a valuable tool for reducing my anxiety.
Regular practice of Box Breath meditation can also help calm the mind, reduce stress and improve focus and concentration. By taking conscious control of your breath, you activate the parasympathetic nervous system, leading to a state of relaxation and balance.

An audio version is available at www.insighttimer.com/saorstudio.

Focus on your breathing to achieve inner calm.

To begin practicing box breath meditation, find a comfortable seated position and follow these steps:

Inhale: Breathe in through your nose and count to four slowly. Allow your belly to expand with each breath. Focus on the sensation of the breath entering and moving through your body.

Hold: Pause and hold your breath for a count of four. Maintain ease in your body during this pause, allowing yourself to be fully present in the moment.

Exhale: Gently and slowly exhale through your mouth for a count of four, emptying your lungs completely. Release any tension or stress with each breath out.

Hold: Once again, hold your breath for a count of four before beginning the next cycle. This pause gives you a moment to gather yourself before proceeding.

Repeat this cycle of inhaling, holding, exhaling, and holding for a few minutes or as long as desired. Focus on the rhythm of your breath and the sensations it creates in your body. This technique can be practiced at any time and location, making it especially helpful during moments of stress or when you need to regain composure.

LOVE NOTE

A Love Note on Embracing Self-Compassion

For years, I allowed myself to be unconsciously conditioned by my surroundings, leading me to believe that success could only be achieved through a relentless pursuit of more. The constant chase to do more, be more, and achieve more harmed my ability to be present, find strength in stillness, and make empowered choices based on knowing rather than reacting.

This unbroken cycle of unconscious reaction stifled my capacity to choose differently. Lost in the endless loop of chasing, I could no longer determine whether my decisions and actions were truly beneficial to me. The lack of awareness kept me trapped in the familiarity of the past, constantly repeating the same patterns.

This relentless chase for more left me overwhelmed and unfulfilled despite my numerous accomplishments. I would often collapse into bed for days or weeks, consumed by a heavy and fearful fog. This constant state of anxiety, panic, and exhaustion left me unable to comprehend how I had ended up in such a place. To cope, I sought ways to numb the painful thoughts. For a long time drinking wine and overeating were my favourite activities to avoid my discomfort.

I discussed this concern with my therapist, and we noticed a recurring pattern. Amidst this unending cycle of constantly seeking perfection, I overlooked the importance of giving myself grace, love, and compassion. I was starting to understand that slowing down held far more power than my current destructive pursuit of more.

Recognizing that my day or week-long crashes were not serving me, I embraced self-compassion. For so long, I'd had abundant love and compassion for others, like the ceaseless flow of sap from a tapped maple tree. Yet, when it came to myself, it seemed nonexistent. The message of "never enough" fuelled my relentless chase for more.

What I swiftly discovered, and what led me to explore compassion more, was the profound realization that self-compassion builds resilience in the face of adversity. Although I still find myself caught up in busyness and occasionally stumble as I navigate this human experience, my newfound understanding has equipped me with the tools to navigate suffering better. Self-compassion sits at the forefront of these tools.

As I feel the urge to rush forward, I remind myself to slow down, engage in mindful activities I love, and allow time for rest. Pausing long enough to listen, I inquire within: What do I truly need? When confronted with discomfort, I gently acknowledge that it also belongs. I encourage myself to be kind within the space of momentary suffering.

To those who, like myself, feel trapped in a relentless chase for more, pause and remember you have the courage to slow down. It is a practice rooted in awareness. Within this newfound awareness, can you choose to love yourself? Embrace joyful activities that fill your resilience cup so that you can face adversity with the knowledge that you are capable of victory. Within the realm of discomfort, allow yourself to recognize that it is a part of your human experience. Pause long enough to observe it with compassion and be kind to yourself as you embark on the journey of growth it offers.

ABUNDANCE

“Do the best you can until you know better. Then, when you know better, do better.”

Maya Angelou

NURTURING AN **ABUNDANT MINDSET**

Awareness of a scarcity mindset is crucial because it greatly influences your thoughts, emotions, and behaviours. A scarcity mindset is characterized by a belief that there is never enough, whether it's money, opportunities, love, or resources. This leads to feelings of fear, anxiety, and competition as you constantly worry about lacking what you need. It restricts your thinking and creativity, making seeing possibilities beyond perceived limitations challenging.

However, cultivating an abundant mindset is empowering. It involves recognizing that there is enough for everyone and that opportunities are limitless. Embracing abundance makes you more open-minded, optimistic, and grateful, fuelling your motivation to take risks, think outside the box, and embrace new opportunities.

Awareness of a scarcity mindset and shifting to an abundant mindset has numerous benefits. It enhances overall well-being and happiness as you focus on gratitude for what you have. It fosters better relationships and collaboration, viewing others' success as opportunities for inspiration and growth. Additionally, an abundant mindset encourages resilience and creativity by fostering resourcefulness and innovative problem-solving. It also enables you to approach setbacks as learning experiences and stepping stones toward future success.

CHARACTERISTICS OF A SCARCITY AND AN ABUNDANT MINDSET:

SCARCITY MINDSET

FEAR OF TAKING RISKS:

Those with a scarcity mindset often hesitate to take risks or try new things because they fear failure or loss. They may stick to their comfort zones and avoid stepping outside of them.

WORRY ABOUT THE FUTURE:

A scarcity mindset tends to generate excessive worry about the future and what might go wrong. A persistent focus on potential negative outcomes leads to anxiety and stress.

COMPARISON AND ENVY:

Individuals with a scarcity mindset often compare themselves to others and feel envious of their success or possessions. They may perceive other people's achievements as a threat to their worth or resources.

RELUCTANCE TO SHARE:

Individuals with a scarcity mindset often compare themselves to others and feel envious of their success or possessions. They may perceive other people's achievements as a threat to their worth or resources.

LACK OF CREATIVITY:

Individuals with a scarcity mindset often compare themselves to others and feel envious of their success or possessions. They may perceive other people's achievements as a threat to their worth or resources.

ABUNDANT MINDSET

OPTIMISM AND POSITIVITY:

People with an abundance mindset tend to have a positive outlook on life. They believe in the potential for growth and see setbacks as learning opportunities than failures.

GRATITUDE AND GENEROSITY:

Those with an abundance mindset express gratitude for what they have and are willing to share their resources, knowledge, and opportunities with others. They understand that giving and receiving creates a positive cycle.

WILLINGNESS TO TAKE RISKS:

An abundance mindset fosters confidence in one's abilities and a willingness to take calculated risks. There is a belief in the availability of opportunities and a readiness to seize them.

COLLABORATION MENTALITY:

Individuals with an abundance mindset value collaboration and cooperation. They recognize that working together can create even greater opportunities and success for everyone involved.

CREATIVE PROBLEM-SOLVING:

An abundance mindset encourages creative thinking and innovation. People are more likely to explore different possibilities and find alternative solutions to challenges.

Reflect on your current attitudes and behaviours regarding your life. Do you tend to focus on what you lack or what you have? How does this perspective influence your overall outlook?

Consider your relationships with others when it comes to sharing resources. Do you often worry about running out, or are you open to giving and receiving? How does this mindset impact your relationships?

Reflect on the language you use when discussing your resources. Do your words lean toward negativity and not enough, or do you frequently express gratitude and having enough?

Describe a situation where you consciously decided to let go of scarcity thinking and embrace abundance instead. How did this change in mindset affect your overall well-being and life?

SUMMARY

Recognizing a scarcity mindset is crucial as it affects your thoughts, emotions, and behaviours. This mindset, characterized by a fear of never having enough, leads to anxiety, competition, and limited thinking. On the other hand, cultivating an abundant mindset allows you to see limitless possibilities and fuels your motivation. Shifting from scarcity to abundance enhances well-being, relationships, resilience, and creativity. By reflecting on your current emotions, you can gain insight into your mindset and choose abundance.

When you find yourself in a scarcity mindset, use the tools presented on the following pages to shift back toward abundance. Employing acts of love and kindness, nurturing forgiveness, and embracing the art of letting go are influential methods for transitioning into an abundant mindset.

CULTIVATE LOVE AND KINDNESS

Love acts as your most extraordinary catalyst when striving to transition from a scarcity mindset to one of abundance. My favourite method for transitioning from fear to faith is through the practice of love and kindness, also known as a "Metta" meditation. This ancient technique entails generating feelings of loving-kindness and extending them toward yourself and others. The roots of this meditation can be traced back to the teachings of Buddhism. Below is a guided meditation that will enable you to experience the power of love and kindness while fostering self-compassion.

An audio version is available at www.insighttimer.com/saorstudio.

Create time to practice love and kindness daily.

Find a comfortable and quiet place to sit. Close your eyes or soften your gaze. Begin by taking a few deep breaths, allowing your body and mind to relax.

Start by directing loving-kindness toward yourself. Repeat silently:

May I be happy.
May I be healthy.
May I be safe.
May I be peaceful and at ease.

As you continue, expand your loving-kindness to others. Picture someone you care about and direct the same phrases toward them:

May you be happy.
May you be healthy.
May you be safe.
May you be peaceful and at ease.

Gradually extend your loving-kindness to include more people, such as friends, family, acquaintances, and even challenging individuals. Repeat the phrases for each person:

May you be happy.
May you be healthy.
May you be safe.
May you be peaceful and at ease.

Finally, extend your loving-kindness to all beings, envisioning a world filled with love and compassion. Repeat the phrases:

May all beings be happy.
May all beings be healthy.
May all beings be safe.
May all beings be peaceful and at ease.

Take a few moments to sit in the feelings of love, kindness, and self-compassion you have cultivated. Practicing this meditation regularly can help develop a sense of self-compassion and empathy toward others. It is a powerful tool for shifting toward an abundance mindset rooted in love and kindness.

THE POWER OF FORGIVENESS AND LETTING GO

Forgiveness is important as it allows you to let go of negative emotions, resentment, and grudges, enabling freedom and peace. It shifts from a scarcity to an abundance mindset, opening up new possibilities. It involves accepting what happened, acknowledging emotions, and releasing attachments to the past. Forgiveness doesn't mean condoning or forgetting actions, but freeing oneself from pain. An example of forgiveness practice is the Hawaiian prayer Ho'oponopono, involving four phrases: "I'm sorry, please forgive me, thank you, I love you." Taking responsibility for experiences and perceptions is key to this practice.

An audio version is available at www.insighttimer.com/saorstudio.

Nurture inner peace through a regular forgiveness practice.

Begin by finding a quiet and comfortable space where you can sit or lie down. Take a few moments to settle into your body, allowing your breath to become slow and steady.

Now, bring to mind someone who has hurt you, or perhaps a mistake or regret that you carry within yourself. Hold this person or situation gently in your mind without judgment.

Take a deep breath in, and as you exhale, silently say to yourself, "I'm sorry." Feel the weight of this apology in your heart as you acknowledge any pain or resentment you may be holding onto.

Now, breathe in again, and as you exhale, say, "Please forgive me." Imagine these words reaching out to the person or situation you seek forgiveness from, opening up a space for healing and understanding.

Take another breath in, and as you exhale, say, "Thank you." Feel a sense of gratitude for the opportunity to grow and learn from this experience, and for the forgiveness that may be granted.

Finally, take a deep breath in, and as you exhale, say, "I love you." Allow love to fill your heart, extending compassion not just to the person or situation you are forgiving, but also to yourself. Embrace the power of love to heal and transform.

I'm sorry.
Please forgive me.
Thank you.
I love you.

With each repetition, feel a sense of release and healing within you.

Take a few more moments to breathe and sit with these feelings of forgiveness and love. When you are ready, gently bring your awareness back to the present moment, feeling a renewed sense of peace and clarity.

Forgiveness is a process that may take time to let go fully. Practice this meditation regularly, and be patient and compassionate with yourself as you navigate your healing journey. May this ancient Hawaiian forgiveness meditation prayer, Ho'oponopono, bring you inner peace and healing.

LOVE NOTE

A Love Note on Shifting Perspectives

After bravely fighting cancer, my father's childhood friend, Ralph, recently passed away. Ralph contributed significantly to his community and fostered multiple children with his wife of over 50 years. Upon hearing this sad news, I immediately called my father to offer my condolences and check on how he was managing. To my surprise, my father happened to be with Ruth, Ralph's wife, and handed the phone to her so I could personally express my sympathies. Ruth's response would profoundly impact me and shift my perspective around loss forever.

"Ruth, I am so sorry for your loss," I said, after hearing her friendly voice.

"What loss, dear?" she replied. "Today, I have not lost anything, but instead gained so much. Ralph is now free from pain and has found the peace he deserves. I gained a lifetime of incredible memories beside him. We have all found comfort and peace now that his suffering has ended." Ruth's words rendered me utterly speechless.

She went on to describe all the things Ralph, and everyone around her had gained on a day that could easily be seen as one of the most difficult days of her life.

In the face of grief, Ruth's uncommon perspective took my breath away. She chose to see the abundance she had gained instead of focusing on what she had lost. This perception did not diminish her love for her husband, nor did it lessen her grief. Rather, it gave her strength to face this challenging day and allowed her and those around her to move forward in the healing process, without feeling overwhelmed or stuck.

I carry this awareness with me as I confront my scarcity mindset and encounter countless opportunities that fuel my belief in "not enough." When I find myself lamenting the end of summer and the limited warm days remaining, I remind myself of the upcoming fall season, the joy it brings with its cooler weather, and the beauty of changing leaves. As I see my children growing up quickly, I shift my perspective to gratitude for the remarkable individuals they are becoming, acknowledging the qualities they have gained through the passage of time. And when I commiserate with friends about another year gone, I choose to remember the wisdom, strength, and courage I have gained as I gracefully age into another year, eagerly embracing the adventures that lie ahead.

Sitting in a mindset of scarcity is not inherently wrong, but I have found that it yields me nothing. Instead, it leaves me feeling paralyzed, unhinged, disoriented, and stuck. I prefer to remember the lesson Ruth taught me and redirect my focus to all I have gained.

Did I lose the summer or gain the wonders of autumn? Did I lose time with my children or gain incredible joy from witnessing their growth? Did I lose my youth or gain the immeasurable wisdom and self-love that comes with age?

Where will you direct your energy? Will you dwell on all you have lost or focus on all you have gained? Take a moment to experience both emotions and notice which one resonates better within your body.

SOUL GOALS

> **"Our deepest fear is that we are powerful beyond measure. It is our light, not our darkness that most frightens us. We ask ourselves, 'Who am I to be brilliant, gorgeous, talented, fabulous?' Actually, who are you not to be?"**
>
> **Marianne Williamson**

AWARENESS

AN INTENTIONAL JOURNEY TOWARD ALIGNMENT

Manifesting goals from a place of authentic desire and what feels good in your body is important as it aligns you with your true self. This alignment taps into the supportive flow of life, attracting opportunities, synchronicities, and resources to help you achieve your goals more readily. When you prioritize what resonates within you, you're living a fulfilling life that isn't dictated by external markers of success. Instead, you focus on your unique path and desires, which leads to greater fulfillment. This alignment also helps you avoid comparison and brings passion and enjoyment to your journey. By manifesting from this place, you attract external support and tap into your own inner resources, enabling you to overcome obstacles and make effective decisions.

Trust the process of aligning with your authentic self and watch as the universe conspires to bring your goals within reach.

Below are five areas of life where it's important to set soul goals:

ENDEAVOURS:

Developing meaningful soul goals involves discovering endeavours that align with your core values. Envision a fulfilling and purpose-driven calling that utilizes your unique abilities and provides an opportunity to support and positively impact your community.

PHYSICAL WELL-BEING:

Setting soul goals for your well-being means prioritizing self-care, health, and overall happiness. It involves listening to your needs, setting intentions for nourishing activities, and cultivating a loving relationship with your physical self.

CONNECTION TO SELF:

Setting soul goals for your spiritual well-being entails fostering a deep connection with the subtle whispers of your inner intuition. This may include practices such as meditation, reflective writing, spending time in nature, or exploring your beliefs and values.

CREATIVITY AND LEARNING:

Setting soul goals in this area encourages you to explore your creative potential and embrace lifelong learning. It involves setting intentions to engage in activities that inspire you, expand your horizons, and allow you to express your enchanted creativity.

RELATIONSHIPS:

Setting soul goals in relationships means cultivating authentic connections and nurturing meaningful bonds. It involves setting intentions to foster healthy communication, empathy, and love in your relationships, whether with a partner, family, friends, or community.

Rate how you currently feel in each of these areas.

ENDEAVOURS

1 2 3 4 5

PHYSICAL WELL-BEING

1 2 3 4 5

CONNECTION TO SELF

1 2 3 4 5

CREATIVITY/LEARNING

1 2 3 4 5

RELATIONSHIPS

1 2 3 4 5

(1 = POORLY and 5 = VERY HAPPY)

ENDEAVOURS:

What core values are important to you, and how can you align your endeavours with them?

What abilities do you possess that can be utilized to make a positive impact in your community?

How can you integrate purpose and meaning into your daily activities to feel more fulfilled?

PHYSICAL WELL-BEING:

How can you prioritize self-care and make it a consistent practice?

What nourishing activities bring you joy and contribute to your overall well-being?

What positive habits can you cultivate to enhance your physical health and happiness?

CONNECTION TO SELF:

What rituals can you incorporate into your daily life to deepen your connection with yourself?

What beliefs are most important to you, and how can you explore your understanding of them?

How can you make space for reflection and self-discovery, such as journaling more often?

CREATIVITY AND LEARNING:

What creative outlets or activities bring you joy? How can you prioritize them in your life?

What new skills do you want to acquire? How can you cultivate lifelong learning?

How can you infuse creativity and learning into different aspects of your life?

RELATIONSHIPS:

What qualities and values do you seek in your relationships?

How can you practice healthy communication, empathy, and love in your relationships?

What actions can you take to nurture and strengthen the meaningful bonds in your life?

How do you want to feel in your life?

Once you have gained awareness of your soul goals, take a moment to consider how achieving these goals will impact how you feel. Consult the Feelings Wheel on page 58 and write the feelings you hope to experience in each quadrant. Once you feel complete, circle the one that aligns most with your aspirations for each category.

ENDEAVOURS

PHYSICAL WELL-BEING

CONNECTION TO SELF

CREATIVITY AND LEARNING

RELATIONSHIPS

Write your desired core feeling in each quadrant below. Make a commitment to base your decisions in these areas of your life on your desired core feelings. Whenever you feel disconnected, take a moment to pause and consider a different path. For example: Will saying "yes" to this experience leave me feeling "blissful" as per my endeavour's soul goal?

ENDEAVOURS

PHYSICAL WELL-BEING

CONNECTION TO SELF

CREATIVITY AND LEARNING

RELATIONSHIPS

Knowing where you are headed is important. By engaging your consciousness, you enable yourself to actively participate in shaping your life. What is your ultimate vision?

Consider your relationships with others when it comes to sharing resources. Do you often worry about running out, or are you open to giving and receiving? How does this mindset impact your relationships?

Consider your values and what matters most to you. What actions or steps can you take to ensure your pathway forward reflects your core values?

Explore your passions and interests. How can you incorporate these into your intentions and goals? How does pursuing what you love contribute to shaping your life?

Reflect on your strengths and unique qualities. How can you leverage these to achieve your intentions and make progress on your pathway forward?

Identify limiting patterns that might hold you back from setting powerful intentions. How can you overcome these barriers and cultivate a mindset that empowers you to create your desired future?

Reflect on past experiences that have brought you joy, growth, or fulfillment. How can you draw from these experiences to set intentions that align with these achievements in life?

Consider the impact you want to have on others. How can your intentions contribute to making a difference? How can you ensure that your path forward positively impacts yourself and others?

Imagine yourself five years from now, having successfully achieved your soul goals, and feeling as you desire. How does that experience make you feel? What steps are necessary to bridge the gap between your current reality and your desired future?

Reflect on the progress you have made so far in shaping your life. Celebrate the steps you have taken and acknowledge your growth. How can you build upon this momentum to continue consciously creating your future?

SUMMARY

Setting soul goals is an incredible way to align with your true self and attract new opportunities. These goals cover five essential areas in your life: endeavours, physical well-being, connection to self, creativity and learning, and relationships. By leveraging your core values and unique abilities, you can bring about a positive impact in your endeavours. Making self-care a priority and recognizing activities that nourish your well-being contributes to your physical health. Connecting with yourself through practices like meditation and spending time in nature strengthens your inner bond. Unlocking your creative potential and embracing a lifelong pursuit of knowledge foster growth and creativity. Nurturing authentic connections, practicing healthy communication, and showing empathy are key to nurturing your relationships.

Utilize the tools in the following pages to further align and commit to your soul goals and deepest desires. Remember, you can make progress every day by cultivating positive thoughts and identifying small tasks that bring you closer to achieving your goals.

ACTION

NURTURE YOUR MENTAL GARDEN

This garden meditation aims to nurture your innate clarity, allowing your dreams to take root and flourish.

As you indulge in this gentle journey of self-exploration, you will discover a renewed sense of inspiration and creativity. The vibrant energy of the garden will infuse your spirit with a zest for life, igniting your imagination and inviting new possibilities to unfold. You will witness the birth of fresh ideas and innovative solutions, as your mind becomes a fertile ground for growth and innovation.

An audio version is available at www.insighttimer.com/saorstudio.

Discover a renewed sense of clarity and perspective.

Take a couple of long, slow breaths and settle into your center. If it feels comfortable, close your eyes and imagine yourself standing in a beautiful garden. Picture the vibrant colours of the flowers, the lush greenery, and the gentle breeze rustling the leaves. Take a moment to soak in the peaceful atmosphere.

As you stroll through the garden, notice a small plot of soil in front of you. This represents your mind, a fertile ground ready to plant seeds of well-being and growth. Visualize yourself holding a handful of seeds, each one representing a different goal or desire you have for yourself.

Take a moment to reflect on these goals and desires. What would you like to cultivate for yourself? Is it self-love, positivity, gratitude, or perhaps a more tangible outcome? Choose one seed at a time and gently plant it into the soil, symbolizing your intention to nurture that particular goal or desire.

Now, imagine a warm beam of sunlight shining down upon the garden. This sunlight represents your love and encouragement toward these thoughts and desires. Feel the warmth and positive energy infusing into the soil, providing nourishment and support for the seeds to grow.

Envision a warm, gentle rain showering the garden, representing you nurturing and caring for these thoughts. Visualize this rainwater seeping into the soil, providing hydration and nourishment to your goals and desires.

As you tend to your mental garden, you also notice some weeds starting to sprout around the planted seeds. These weeds represent negative thoughts or doubts that may hinder the growth of your efforts. Take a moment to pluck each weed from the soil, symbolizing your commitment to removing negativity and embracing a positive mindset.

Notice, over time, as the seeds sprout and grow into healthy plants. See them reaching toward the sky, their vibrant colours and beautiful blossoms reflecting your progress and growth over time. Observe the transformation within yourself as you continue to nurture these thoughts of love and kindness toward yourself. What does it feel like to witness this growth you dreamed for yourself?

Imagine your garden in full bloom. Imagine yourself surrounded by a flourishing oasis of wellbeing. Feel the joy and fulfillment that comes from caring for your mental garden and witnessing your goals and desires come to fruition.

When you are ready, slowly open your eyes and carry the peaceful energy of your mental garden with you into the world. Remember to revisit this meditation whenever you need to reconnect with your goals and deepest desires.

ACTION

BRIDGING THE GAP BETWEEN SOMEDAY AND TODAY

Take a moment to pause and consider what you would like to achieve today. For instance, doing laundry, preparing lunches, responding to emails, etc. Write each task down in the TODAY column.

Next, take a moment to envision your long-term aspirations. Write down your most ambitious goals in the SOMEDAY column and feel free to dream big.

TODAY	SOMEDAY

Now, compare the two lists. Can you identify any items on your TODAY list that will propel you toward achieving items on your SOMEDAY list? Many individuals would respond “no” to this question. Consider what could happen if you started including more modest tasks on your TODAY list that could gradually bring you closer to your SOMEDAY dreams.

LOVE NOTE

A Love Note on Reclaiming My Purpose

I was one of those individuals who had a meticulously-crafted plan. I had a five-year and ten year plan, and I was determined to make it all happen. By the time I reached my thirties, I had achieved what society would consider great success. I had the privilege of working at top-tier brands like Pepsi and Gatorade and leading the women's category at Nike Canada. I was happily married and welcomed two beautiful children into my life. It seemed as though I was living the dream. However, despite ticking off all the boxes, my anxiety was skyrocketing and my mental health hit a new low. I couldn't understand why. I had followed my plan dutifully, so why wasn't I happy?

During this period, I realized the goals I had set for myself were not driven by what I truly needed and desired, but rather by the expectations of others. I had been influenced by what I thought I needed for external validation, rather than setting goals based on my own desires. So, my husband and I decided to save money and set aside enough to allow me to stay home with our children for two years. By eliminating the cost of daycare and utilizing our savings, we could live comfortably while I took the time to reevaluate my goals, take care of myself and our small family. This time, I wanted to set goals aligned with how I wanted to feel, rather than conforming to societal expectations.

While at home with the kids, I started incorporating more exercise into my routine. I delved into certifications that would enhance my understanding of movement and help me uncover why physical exercise had such a positive impact on my mental health. That's how I found myself in a barre certification program, surrounded by dancers who were twenty years younger than me. I felt completely out of place. Like a baby learning to walk for the first time, I stumbled and fell more than I walked. There were moments when I almost quit, but I persevered and dedicated myself to practicing for my certification exam. I invited my neighbours into my backyard so I could practice with a group.

My motivation for exercise was not losing weight or fitting into a certain image; I taught from a place of wanting to feel good, not look good. It felt vulnerable and uncomfortable, but I began to realize I wasn't alone. Movement was helping others feel better, just as it did for me. This realization fuelled my passion, and I pursued additional certifications, constantly seeking to expand my knowledge and discover new ways to move the body to open the heart.

As my backyard became too small to accommodate everyone, I decided to rent space at a local dance studio. Some of my class participants, who shared similar experiences, expressed their interest in teaching. I willingly shared everything I had learned and invited them to teach alongside me. Fast forward five years, and I never returned to my corporate job. I had saved enough money to open my own studio, where I teach movement, not based on society's expectations but according to our community's shared values. We move our bodies to shift our minds and open our hearts. I feel more fulfilled, and I no longer make rigid five-year plans. Instead, I tune into what I need and how I want to feel, and I plan my life accordingly.

ADDITIONAL TOOLS

AWARENESS

TOOLS THAT HELP YOU **FEEL GOOD**

The tools in this section are designed to help you feel good. They provide opportunities for self-reflection and can shift your inner narrative. There are days when I simply don't feel good and struggle to grasp the reasons behind it. In the past, I would get caught up in trying to identify what went wrong and what I could do to regain my happier self. However, I have grown to appreciate that there will be those days, when answers may not be readily available, and solutions may not be within reach. During these times, I open myself to the discomfort I feel and allow it to be part of me. And when I'm ready, I use the tools provided in this section to lift myself up and move forward. Because I do believe that, no matter the circumstances, there is always a pathway forward.

“Self-care is giving the world the best of you, instead of what is left of you.”

Katie Reed

ACTION

EMBRACE THE MAGIC OF GRATITUDE

Gratitude is often praised as a popular wellness practice, and for good reason—it truly works. Engaging in gratitude can be a wonderful experience that brings about positive emotions. Numerous research studies have demonstrated that gratitude enhances emotional, physical, and mental well-being. It improves your sleep, boosts your creativity, and sharpens your decisionmaking abilities, among a myriad of other advantages.

Robert Emmons asserts that gratitude allows you to fully recognize the value of something, enabling you to derive even more benefits from it. When you deeply appreciate something, you are less likely to take it for granted.

To fully reap the rewards of a regular gratitude practice, it is important to move beyond mere thoughts of gratitude and take a moment to genuinely experience the emotions it invokes.

Reflect on something that you are extremely grateful for today and explain why it holds so much value in your life. I could be a person, place or thing.

Write about a recent experience that made you feel grateful and describe how it positively impacted your well-being.

Take a moment to appreciate a personal relationship that has brought joy and positivity to your life, and explain why it is significant to you.

Write about a challenge or obstacle you recently faced and identify something within the situation that you can be grateful for, even if it was a lesson learned or personal growth achieved.

Reflect upon something in your life that you often take for granted, and describe the feelings of gratitude that arise when you truly appreciate its presence.

ACTION

THE ART OF HOLDING SPACE

I used to feel uncomfortable witnessing someone's distress and would try to rescue them with advice. However, I realized that I was projecting my own experiences onto them and not leaving space for them to feel what was present within themselves. Thankfully, I discovered the true art of holding space, which involves being present for others physically, mentally, and emotionally. This has proven to be a much more powerful tool in helping people I love.

When you listen attentively and ask open-ended questions, you create a safe space for individuals to explore their thoughts and emotions. This empowers them to trust themselves and find their own answers. Your role is to provide a non-judgmental environment for them to uncover their own truth and grow.

Holding space instead of rescuing individuals can have several benefits:

Reflect on current relationships where you excel at holding space. Consider the positive effects these individuals have experienced.

EMPOWERMENT:

By allowing individuals to find their answers, you empower them to tap into their own wisdom and capabilities. This fosters self-reliance, self-confidence, and a sense of personal agency.

OWNERSHIP AND ACCOUNTABILITY:

When individuals are given the space to find their own answers, they take ownership of their decisions and actions. This promotes personal growth, resilience, and a sense of responsibility.

INCREASED SELF-AWARENESS:

Holding space for individuals to figure things out on their own encourages self-reflection and introspection. This can lead to greater self-understanding and personal growth.

SUSTAINABLE SOLUTIONS:

Allowing individuals to find their own answers often results in solutions tailored to their specific needs and goals. These solutions tend to be more sustainable and effective in the long run.

STRENGTHENED RELATIONSHIPS:

By holding space for individuals to find their own answers, you demonstrate trust and respect for their abilities and autonomy. This fosters mutual support, understanding, and collaboration.

LEARNING OPPORTUNITIES:

By refraining from rescuing and allowing individuals to figure things out on their own, the listener can learn from the other person's thought process, insights, and problem-solving skills. This facilitates personal growth and development.

Here are some examples of how a listener can actively hold space for someone:

As you read through them, take a moment to think about existing relationships where you may demonstrate these behaviours.

NON-JUDGMENTAL ATTITUDE:

The listener approaches the conversation with an open mind, suspending preconceived notions. They refrain from making assumptions or passing judgment on the speaker's thoughts, feelings, or experiences.

ACTIVE PRESENCE:

The listener is fully present, giving their undivided attention. They maintain eye contact, use open body language, and provide cues to demonstrate engagement and attentiveness.

CLARIFYING QUESTIONS:

Instead of offering their own opinions, the listener asks open-ended questions to encourage deeper exploration of thoughts and feelings. These questions help the speaker gain clarity, explore different angles, and discover their own insights and solutions.

EMPATHY AND VALIDATION:

The listener seeks to understand the speaker's perspective and emotions. They acknowledge the speaker's feelings and experiences, validating them without dismissing or minimizing their significance.

PROVIDE SPACE FOR SILENCE:

The listener recognizes the power of silence, allowing pauses for reflection and processing. They avoid filling gaps with their advice, allowing the speaker to express themselves fully and at their own pace.

NON-INTERRUPTIVE AND ATTENTIVE:

The listener refrains from interrupting or diverting the conversation to their own experiences. They avoid distractions, such as checking their phone, to show respect and genuine interest in the speaker's narrative.

Here are examples of different types of listeners who fail to hold space:

As you read through them, take a moment to think about existing relationships where you may demonstrate these behaviours.

THE DISTRACTED LISTENER:

This listener is constantly preoccupied with thoughts, distractions, or technology, which hinders engagement and connection.

THE KNOW-IT-ALL LISTENER:

This listener dominates conversations with their own opinions or experiences, making others feel dismissed or invalidated.

THE RESCUE LISTENER:

This listener immediately jumps in to offer advice or solutions without fully understanding the speaker's situation or needs, undermining autonomy and hindering selfexpression.

THE SELECTIVE LISTENER:

This listener pays attention only to certain parts of what the speaker is saying, disregarding other aspects and leading to misunderstanding.

THE SELF-CENTERED LISTENER:

This listener constantly redirects the conversation to themselves, disregarding the speaker's feelings and experiences.

THE PROSECUTOR LISTENER:

This listener approaches conversations with a critical or judgmental mindset, creating a defensive atmosphere and damaging trust.

THE REHEARSING LISTENER:

This listener focuses more on formulating their own reply instead of genuinely understanding the speaker's words, diminishing the depth of connection.

THE DEFENSIVE LISTENER:

This listener becomes defensive or argumentative in response to the speaker's words, focusing on defending their perspective rather than empathizing with the speaker.

Reflect on a recent conversation where you displayed one of the listener types that does not hold space for a speaker. What was your role in that conversation? How did your behaviour affect the speaker's experience? How might you have improved your listening?

Think about a time when you felt truly heard and seen by someone. What qualities did that person exhibit as a listener? How did it make you feel? How can you incorporate those qualities into your listening style?

Consider a relationship where you tend to default to a specific listening style that does not hold space for the other. What underlying motivations or beliefs might be driving this behaviour? How can you challenge those beliefs and approach the situation with a more open and supportive mindset?

Imagine a scenario where someone is sharing a problem or seeking guidance. How can you create a safe and generous space for them to explore their thoughts and find solutions? What specific actions or behaviours can you practice to cultivate this type of listening?

Reflect on your own self-awareness and ability to hold space for yourself. How can developing a deeper understanding of your own thoughts, emotions, and needs help you become a more generous listener? How does self-compassion affect your ability to hold space for others?

CULTIVATE COMPASSION THROUGH SELF-LOVE

Self-love is the practice of caring for and valuing yourself unconditionally. It involves treating yourself with kindness, compassion, and respect, just as you would treat a dear friend. Self-love is important because it forms the foundation for your overall well-being and happiness. When you genuinely love and accept yourself, you can experience more fulfilling relationships, better physical and mental health, and greater personal growth.

Louise Hay, a renowned author, speaker, and teacher, dedicated her life's work to emphasizing the power of positive affirmations and the practice of self-love as catalysts for healing and personal development.

In my late twenties, I stumbled upon an audio of Louise Hay discussing self-love. Her words were refreshingly simple yet powerful, altering my inner dialogue and inspiring empathy and compassion. I still pass on these valuable lessons, eager to share the impact they had on me.

How to cultivate self-love according to Louise Hay.

1. STOP CRITICIZING YOURSELF:

Instead of focusing on your flaws and mistakes, choose to acknowledge your strengths and achievements.

2. LET GO OF NEGATIVE SELF-TALK:

Replace self-criticism with positive and empowering self-talk. Speak to yourself with kindness, as you would to a dear friend.

3. RELEASE TOXIC RELATIONSHIPS:

Surround yourself with people who uplift and support you, and let go of relationships that drain your energy or bring you down.

4. LET GO OF THE PAST:

Release any past pain, regrets, or resentment that may be holding you back. Focus on the present moment and create a positive future for yourself.

5. STOP COMPARING:

Each person's journey is unique, so comparing yourself to others only leads to unnecessary self-doubt. Embrace your individuality.

6. LET GO OF SELF-JUDGMENT:

Release the habit of constantly judging yourself and embrace selfacceptance. Remember that you are worthy of love and compassion.

7. STOP NEGLECTING YOUR NEEDS:

Prioritize self-care and ensure you meet your physical, emotional, and spiritual needs. Nurturing yourself is essential for self-love.

8. STOP SEEKING PERFECTION:

Embrace your imperfections and recognize that they make you unique. Allow yourself to make mistakes and learn from them.

9. PRACTICE FORGIVENESS:

Forgive yourself for past mistakes and let go of any resentment or grudges you hold against yourself. Forgiveness allows for healing and growth.

10. STOP SEEKING APPROVAL:

Relying on external validation can be draining. Instead, learn to trust yourself and follow your inner guidance.

Use the journal prompts to help you inspire more self-love while applying Louise Hay's strategies. Consistency, genuine belief, and intention are key factors in improving the effectiveness of this practice.

SELF-CRITICISM

In what area of your life do you tend to be self-critical? Take a moment to shift your perspective and write down three qualities that you genuinely appreciate about yourself.

NEGATIVE SELF-TALK

Pay attention to your inner dialogue for a few moments. Write down any negative self-talk you notice and challenge it with positive, affirming statements.

TOXIC RELATIONSHIPS

Identify a relationship that drains your energy and write about ways to establish boundaries or distance yourself from that person.

LETTING GO OF THE PAST

Write a letter to your past self, acknowledging the pain or regrets you carry. Reflect on how you can release them and focus on building a positive future.

COMPARISON

Identify an area of your life where you tend to compare yourself to others. Journal about your unique strengths and why it's important that you are different.

SELF-JUDGMENT

Explore a situation where you were hard on yourself. Write about how you can offer yourself compassion and understanding instead.

NEGLECTING NEEDS

List three self-care activities you enjoy and commit to incorporating them into your routine regularly. Reflect on how they make you feel.

SEEKING PERFECTION

Recall a time when you felt pressured to be perfect. Journal about how embracing imperfections can lead to personal growth and self-acceptance

FORGIVENESS

Reflect on a mistake or regret that you hold onto. Write a forgiveness letter to yourself, expressing understanding and releasing any self-blame.

SEEKING APPROVAL

Describe where you seek external validation in your life. Reflect on how you can honour your own desires and values moving forward.

THE POWER OF POSITIVE AFFIRMATIONS

A positive affirmation is a purposely-crafted phrase that aims to uplift and empower oneself. It serves as a means of reprogramming the subconscious mind with optimistic thoughts and beliefs. I incorporate affirmations into my daily routine. I naturally gravitate toward thoughts that anticipate negative outcomes, so I work on shifting my perspective by repeating positive affirmations. In moments of fear, I respond with "I am safe" in my mind. When facing challenges that seem overwhelming, I reinforce my confidence with the mantra "I am ready. I can and I will overcome this obstacle."

Regardless of any negative thoughts that attempt to hinder my progress and discourage me from moving forward, I rely on positive affirmations to provide the support and motivation necessary to navigate discomfort and forge ahead.

By creating your own positive affirmations and repeating them often, you can experience several benefits:

SHIFT IN MINDSET:

Affirmations help to shift your mindset from negative or limiting beliefs to more positive and empowering ones. They can help you replace self-doubt, fear, and selfcriticism with self-confidence, self-love, and self-acceptance.

INCREASED SELF-BELIEF:

Affirmations can boost your self-esteem. By consistently affirming positive qualities and abilities, you reinforce a positive self-image and develop a stronger sense of self-worth.

IMPROVED FOCUS:

Regularly repeating affirmations can help you stay focused on your goals and aspirations. They serve as reminders of what you want to achieve and can provide the motivation and determination to pursue them.

STRESS REDUCTION:

Positive affirmations can help reduce stress and anxiety by promoting a more positive and optimistic outlook. They can counteract negative thoughts and replace them with feelings of calmness, peace, and resilience.

ENHANCED SELF-CARE:

Affirmations encourage self-care and self-nurturing. They remind you to prioritize your well-being, practice self-love, and take care of your physical, emotional, and mental health.

ATTRACTION OF ABUNDANCE:

Affirmations help you manifest prosperity by aligning your thoughts with the energy of abundance. They can help you develop a positive mindset and attract opportunities.

IMPROVED RELATIONSHIPS:

Affirmations can positively impact your relationships by promoting selflove, compassion, and forgiveness. They can also help you attract and maintain healthy, loving, and supportive relationships.

INCREASED RESILIENCE:

Regularly practicing positive affirmations can build resilience and help you bounce back from setbacks or challenges. They can remind you of your strengths, capabilities, and the power within you to overcome obstacles.

What negative beliefs or self-talk do you often engage in? Write down any self-critical thoughts or limiting beliefs that you frequently experience.

How do these negative beliefs or self-talk affect your life? Reflect on the impact these thoughts have on your self-esteem, relationships, goals, and overall well-being.

What positive qualities or affirmations do you desire to embody? Identify the positive qualities, beliefs, and attitudes you want to cultivate.

What evidence or experiences in your life support these positive qualities? Recall instances where you have demonstrated or experienced the positive qualities you desire.

How can you reframe your negative beliefs into positive affirmations? Take each negative belief or self-talk and rewrite it in a positive, empowering manner.

How can you make these affirmations more personal and impactful? Customize the affirmations to align with your goals, values, and circumstances. Make them resonate deeply with you.

How can you integrate these affirmations into your daily life? Explore ways to incorporate the affirmations into your daily routine, such as repeating them in the morning, writing them on sticky notes, or creating a vision board.

How can you reinforce these affirmations with daily actions of self-love? Reflect on the steps you can take to align with your affirmations. Consider how you can practice self-care, set boundaries, or move toward your goals.

Write out your final list of positive affirmations that resonate deeply with you below and commit to reading or repeating them to yourself each day. Affirmations are most effective when personalized, heartfelt, and specific to your experiences and desires.

Here are positive affirmations by Louise Hay for inspiration:

1. I am willing to release old beliefs that no longer serve me.
2. I am deserving of love and happiness.
3. I choose to fill my mind with positive and uplifting thoughts.
4. I am grateful for all the abundance in my life.
5. I trust that everything happens for my highest good.
6. I am safe, secure, and protected at all times.
7. I am open to receiving miracles and blessings.
8. I am deserving of all the good things life has to offer.
9. I am willing to forgive and let go of past hurts.
10. I am grateful for the lessons I've learned and the growth I've experienced.
11. I am surrounded by love and support.
12. I am capable of creating a life filled with joy and fulfillment.
13. I am confident in my ability to make positive changes in my life.
14. I am worthy of love, respect, and kindness.
15. I am grateful for my body and treat it with love and care.
16. I am abundant in all areas of my life.
17. I trust in the process of life and know that everything is working out for me.
18. I release all fear and embrace the power within me.
19. I am open to receiving love and giving love freely.
20. I am grateful for the present moment and live fully in it.
21. I am deserving of success and prosperity.
22. I am worthy of living a life filled with passion and purpose.
23. I am surrounded by positive and supportive people.
24. I am capable of achieving my goals and dreams.

25. I am connected to the wisdom of the universe.
26. I am grateful for all the opportunities that come my way.
27. I am free from the past and fully focused on the present.
28. I am deserving of all the good that comes into my life.
29. I am grateful for the abundance that flows to me effortlessly.
30. I trust my intuition and make decisions with clarity and confidence.
31. I am loved and cherished for who I am.
32. I am willing to release old patterns and embrace new, positive ones.
33. I am worthy of self-care and prioritize my well-being.
34. I am grateful for the beauty and joy that surrounds me.
35. I am confident in expressing my true self authentically.
36. I am deserving of peace and harmony in all areas of my life.
37. I am open to receiving all the blessings that are meant for me.
38. I am grateful for the lessons learned from past experiences.
39. I am capable of achieving anything I set my mind to.
40. I am worthy of unconditional love and acceptance.
41. I am grateful for my unique gifts and talents.
42. I release any need for comparison and embrace my own journey.
43. I am deserving of happiness and fulfillment.
44. I am connected to the infinite wisdom within me.
45. I am grateful for the love and support that surrounds me.
46. I am confident in my ability to overcome challenges.
47. I am open to receiving abundance in all forms.
48. I am worthy of living a life that brings me joy and satisfaction.
49. I am grateful for the opportunities that help me grow and evolve.
50. I am deserving of all the good that life has in store for me.

LIVING A MEANINGFUL LIFE

Funerals are a source of wonder as people come together to celebrate the departed's impact on their lives. I have always observed that career achievements or professional successes are rarely mentioned during these occasions of reflection. Instead, the focus remains on the departed's role as a loving parent, a devoted partner, or a true friend. The memories shared revolve around the joy they brought, the obstacles they helped overcome, and the constant support and encouragement they provided. This raises the question of why so many people still dedicate so much time and energy solely to their careers and professional advancement.

In his book The Road to Character, David Brooks explores the distinction between resume and eulogy virtues. Resume virtues refer to the skills, achievements, and accolades that are often highlighted on a traditional resume. They are the external markers of success that society recognizes and values.

On the other hand, eulogy virtues are the qualities, values, and character traits that define who you truly are and how you have lived your life. These virtues are spoken about in your eulogy, reflecting the impact you had on others and the legacy you leave behind.

Brooks argues that while society often focuses on developing and showcasing your resume virtues, cultivating your eulogy virtues truly brings fulfillment and meaning. These virtues include empathy, kindness, integrity, courage, and compassion. They are the qualities that shape your relationships, define your character, and contribute to the betterment of yourself and the world around you.

Resume virtues are important and bring external recognition and success; however, it is the cultivation of eulogy virtues that leads to a life of meaning, purpose, and genuine fulfillment.

Use the journal prompts on the next page to explore and develop the eulogy virtues that resonate with you, and begin shaping your life around them.

Reflect on the times you prioritized your resume virtues over your eulogy virtues. How did this affect your overall satisfaction and sense of fulfillment?

Identify three eulogy virtues that you deeply value and would like to cultivate further. How can you incorporate these virtues into your daily life and interactions with others?

Consider a person you admire who embodies strong eulogy virtues. What specific qualities do they possess? How can you further emulate those virtues in your own life?

Reflect on a time when you made a decision based on your eulogy virtues, even if it went against societal expectations. How did this decision align with your values and sense of purpose?

Write a eulogy for yourself, focusing on the eulogy virtues you would like to be remembered for. How can you start living in alignment with those virtues today?

ACTION

ACCESS MORE JOY

Knowing what brings you joy, especially the small and seemingly insignificant things, is important because it allows you to cultivate a sense of happiness, contentment, and fulfillment in your daily life.

Consciously appreciating small joys can shift your focus from waiting for significant achievements to finding contentment and happiness in your daily life. By exploring and celebrating these little joys, you can experience a profound impact, infusing life with wonder and fulfillment.

Here are five benefits you may experience by prioritizing simple moments of joy in your day.

INCREASED WELL-BEING:

Engaging in activities that bring joy boosts your mood, reduces stress, and enhances your mental and emotional state. You create a ripple of positivity throughout your day by consciously seeking out and appreciating the little moments of joy, such as enjoying an uninterrupted coffee.

MINDFULNESS AND PRESENCE:

Recognizing and savouring small joys encourages you to be present in the moment. It helps you cultivate mindfulness as you become fully aware of the simple pleasures and find gratitude in them. This practice grounds you in the present and allows you to fully experience and appreciate the richness of life.

SELF-CARE AND PRIORITIZATION:

Knowing what brings you joy helps you prioritize self-care. It reminds you to take time for yourself and engage in activities that nourish your soul. By consciously making space for joy, you prioritize your happiness and well-being, which ultimately benefits you and those around you.

INNER ALIGNMENT:

Discovering and embracing what brings you joy is an exploration of your authentic self. It helps you align your actions and choices with your true desires and values. When you prioritize joy, you align with your inner truth, leading to a more fulfilling and purpose-driven life.

INSPIRATION AND MOTIVATION:

The awareness of what brings you joy can serve as a source of inspiration and motivation. When you know what lights you up, you can intentionally seek out or incorporate those experiences into your daily routine. This fuels your enthusiasm, creativity, and passion, energizing and motivating you to pursue your goals and dreams.

Create a budget-friendly list of twenty small activities that bring you joy and commit to engaging in one for 20 minutes each day for the next 20 days.

1
2
3
4
5
6
7
8
9
10
11
12
13
14
15
16
17
18
19
20

MOVEMENT FOR HEALING

Incorporating movement into your daily routine offers many benefits. It promotes physical well-being and enhances mental and emotional health. When you exercise, your body releases a wonderful chemical concoction that contributes to an overall sense of happiness. This concoction includes: endorphins, which alleviate pain and induce a sense of euphoria; dopamine, which amplifies pleasure and reward; serotonin, which lifts mood and reduces anxiety; and more. These chemicals are released as a response to physical activity and can have a lasting positive impact on your overall health.

Here are three ways to introduce movement into your life.

EMBRACE FREE MOVEMENT:

Engaging in unconstrained movement serves as an enjoyable and expressive art form and holds immense therapeutic value. Whether you partake in free-movement efforts alone or in a group, this practice enables you to release buried emotions, boost self-confidence, and foster a deeper connection with your body. Choose a free-movement technique that resonates with you, turn up your favourite song, and let your body sway to its own rhythm.

IMMERSE YOURSELF IN NATURE:

Sometimes, the healing power of movement lies in immersing yourself in the tranquility of nature. Taking a leisurely walk or embarking on a scenic hike can be wonderfully rejuvenating. Utilize this opportunity to be fully present, observe your surroundings, and pay attention to the sensations in your body as you move.

GROUP FITNESS:

Participating in group fitness classes has significant mental health benefits. Being active in a group creates a sense of community and connection. Peer support uplifts and motivates, combating feelings of loneliness or isolation. Group fitness classes also provide structure and routine, which is valuable for those with mental health conditions like depression or anxiety. Join the SAOR community for a class anytime, virtually or in person. Details can be found at www.saorstudio.com/freeclass

The combination of exercise, nature, and social support greatly improves mental well-being. Remember that these suggestions are merely starting points, and you can always tailor them to meet your specific needs and preferences. The key is to discover activities that resonate with you and bring you genuine joy while allowing your body to move freely.

THE HEALING POWER OF SOUND

Sound, as a form of expression and healing, has deep roots in ancient cultures and spiritual traditions. These practices acknowledge the profound impact that sound vibrations can have on your physical, mental, and emotional well-being.

These exercises involve intentional sound expression to connect with higher states of consciousness, promote self-healing, and cultivate overall well-being. The vibrations created through vocalization have the potential to cleanse and harmonize your energetic body, release emotional blockages, and induce a sense of calm. Regular practice of sound expression exercises can enhance self-awareness, alleviate stress, and support physical and emotional health.

Here are three exercises that can help express sound and energy:

MANTRA CHANTING

(Origin: Hinduism and Buddhism)

Exercise:
Choose a sacred mantra or chant, such as "Om" or "Om Mani Padme Hum." Sit comfortably and repeat the chosen mantra aloud or silently.

Benefits:
Mantra chanting aids in focusing the mind, inducing a meditative state, and fostering inner peace. Additionally, it can improve concentration, alleviate anxiety, and promote spiritual connection.

TONING

(Origin: Indigenous and Shamanic Traditions):

Exercise:
Stand or sit in a relaxed position. Take a deep breath and release a sustained vocal tone, such as "ah" or "oh," allowing the sound to resonate within your body.

Benefits:
Toning assists in releasing emotional blockages, restoring energetic balance, and encouraging self-expression. Furthermore, it can enhance body awareness, boost vocal confidence, and increase overall vitality.

HUMMING BEE BREATH

(Origin: Kundalini yoga):

Exercise:
Sit comfortably and close your eyes. Gently place your index fingers in your ears, allowing the remaining fingers to rest lightly on your face. Inhale deeply, and as you exhale, create a humming sound resembling that of a bee. Feel the vibration of the sound resonating throughout your head and body.

Benefits:
This practice aids in calming the mind, alleviating anxiety, and promoting relaxation. Additionally, it can enhance concentration and focus.

A LETTER FROM WITHIN

You have just discovered a wealth of insight about your limiting patterns and how you can rewrite them to empower yourself. You gained a deeper understanding of your emotions, learned to set boundaries that protect your needs, experienced mindfulness tools to help you stay focused, and discovered ways to support your nervous system during this transitional period. Additionally, you have learned how to shift into abundance whenever you find yourself slipping back into old ways as you continue on this journey of self-discovery.

I invite you to imagine yourself one year from now and write a letter as your future self. Reflect on the remarkable transformation you have undergone. What new insights have you uncovered? Recall any setbacks you encountered along the way and how you overcame them. As you write, embrace the person you have become with all this newfound awareness and take pride in the actions you have taken over the past year.

I encourage you to engage in this powerful exercise of speaking from the perspective of your future-self. By envisioning yourself as having already achieved your desired outcome, you open yourself up energetically to the possibility of its manifestation. This exercise also prepares you to embrace discomfort, as you now have a clear understanding of the wonderful rewards awaiting you on the other side.

Once you have written your letter, read it aloud to someone who will hold you accountable on this journey. Sharing your aspirations and commitments with a trusted individual will provide you with support and guidance along the way.

This is a journey of growth and change. Embrace the insights you have uncovered so far, and trust that you are capable of creating the life you desire.

“The greatest glory in living lies not in never falling, but in rising every time we fall.”

Nelson Mandela

Book Recommendations

Books are one of my preferred methods for learning and personal growth. I love audio books, which allow me to listen during dog walks, long drives, or gardening. Here are some of my top book recommendations to support your ongoing work.

The Untethered Soul, Michael Singer

The Go-Giver, Bob Burg and John David Mann

How To Do The Work, Nicole LePera

The Body is Not an Apology, Sonya Renee Taylor

It's Not Always Depression, Diana Fosha

You Can Heal Your Life, Louise Hay

The Power of Now, Eckhart Tolle

Anatomy of the Spirit, Caroline Myss

Think Indigenous, Doug Good Feather

Man's Search for Meaning, Victor Frankl

The Four Agreements, Don Miguel Ruiz

What Happened To You?, Oprah Winfrey and Bruce D. Perry

Stolen Focus, Johann Hari

Journey to the Heart, Melody Beattie

Trusting the Gold, Tara Brach

Art of Possibility, Rosamund Stone Zander

Light is the New Black, Rebecca Campbell

Atlas of the Heart, Brené Brown

In The Flo, Alisa Vitti

The Joy of Movement, Kelly McGonigal

Relax and Renew, Judith Hanson Lasater

Scattered Minds, Gabor Maté

Breath: The New Science of a Lost Art, James Nestor

“I can and I will.”

The celebrated mantra
of every SAOR member.

About the Author

Nathania Harrison (Nat) is a dedicated and passionate advocate for mental health, striving to eliminate the stigma surrounding it. As the founder and owner of SAOR, a thriving mindful movement studio in Toronto, she has created a safe space for women to move their bodies, shift their minds, and access an open-heart state of calm and contentment.

With a background in marketing and brand management for companies like Pepsi and Nike, Nat brings a solid business foundation to her entrepreneurial efforts. She is a lifelong learner, constantly seeking new ways to connect within and share her experiences with others.

Nat's dedication to personal growth extends beyond marketing and the studio. As a multiple Ironman and marathon finisher, she understands the transformative power of hard work, both physically and mentally. She believes vulnerability is essential for meaningful connection and is committed to helping others, like her, who desire more.

“It takes courage to grow up and become who you really are.”

e.e. cummings

Gratitude from the Author

This workbook would not be possible without the incredible support of so many individuals. Firstly, I would like to express my deepest gratitude to my husband, Mark, whose unwavering belief in my abilities has been instrumental in bringing my ideas to life. During low moments of self-doubt and imposter syndrome, he has lifted me up, brushed me off, and reminded me of the direction I am heading.

I am grateful to my children, who possess immense creativity and have inspired me to fearlessly embrace terrible first drafts and persist even when the odds seemed insurmountable. Their dedication to trying new things and relentless practice to be better serve as my guiding light, teaching me the importance of embracing a beginner's mindset.

To my parents and mother-in-law, I extend my heartfelt appreciation for your constant support with my busy family, enabling space for me to focus on my work and complete this book. I am eternally grateful to my mom and dad for their unwavering support in helping me overcome many mental health obstacles, never allowing them to defeat me or define me.

I am forever indebted to Sylvia, who has been with me since the inception of this endeavour. She recognized the potential of Return To You and has dedicated countless hours, as my energetic partner, providing unwavering support and ensuring that tangible steps were taken to foster the growth and success of this program and workbook.

My utmost gratitude extends to the entire SAOR team of trainers and staff. The creation of SAOR has undeniably been a collaborative effort, fuelled by your boundless love and energy. Your unwavering commitment and dedication have afforded me the space to create this workbook. Thank you for consistently going above and beyond.

I want to express my deepest appreciation to our SAOR community. Your presence has provided me with a safe and nurturing space where I can explore, evolve, and engage in this work. Your unwavering support has allowed me to embrace vulnerability, messiness, and discomfort, allowing for my personal growth and transformation. I am truly grateful for the immense support you have offered and continue to provide.

Lastly, I extend my thanks to my mastermind group and dear friends, who have never questioned my pursuit of mental health and well-being. Thank you for standing by me, nourishing my spirit, challenging my ridgid boundaries, sharing dreams, and embarking on this journey alongside me as I navigate life's bumpy roads.

“You never feel like it, and you never regret it.”

Nat Harrison

Manufactured by Amazon.ca
Bolton, ON